Why Hypnosis for Personal Development

How to Re-Script Our Life Script with Hypnosis, How to Manage Our Thoughts and Behaviors by Our Emotions, and How to Use Our Dreams to Find Our Answers

Susanna Safa

contained within this document, including, but not limited to, errors, omissions, or inaccuracies.

Table of Contents

Disclaimer

All the information contained in this book is only for your information purposes. This information should not be used to substitute professional diagnosis, advice, or treatment. You should always visit your practitioner with questions you have regarding a particular medical condition.

Hypnotherapy products and services do not diagnose or cure disease. They are natural products or services, and they act as complementary healing arts. Use the information as instructed, and if you require medical advice, diagnosis, or treatment, please speak to your doctor.

Introduction

There are two ways you can survive in this world, but only one way can help you succeed. The holy grail of success lies within the art of being in full control of your mind. Without mastering our minds, we're mere puppets, playing out the scenes of someone else's story. By learning to conquer the mind, the world becomes your puppet, allowing you to design any story you desire.

Figure One

A fact you can't escape is that the world is changing, and some days you may not think you have what it takes to adapt to the changes. You've always had a dream, a wish to see your life head in a certain direction. This direction is strongly dependent on your beliefs and desires, and it isn't always clear from where these beliefs came. You're often left to wonder how your life has come to what it is now, and how you can change it to something you desire. This usually follows a realization that you don't always desire what you did some time ago. That's because your eyes can open, making you question everything you think, feel, and do.

You begin to question why you do the things you do. Why do you smoke? Why do you drink? For what reason do you perceive the world as it is? How have you come to feel like you're always on edge, and one step closer to becoming a rigid stress ball? These are some questions we start asking ourselves when we have no memory of what brought us to this point. We had no control and continue to navigate this crazy world with everything it throws our way without giving it a second thought. Once you start questioning reality, your behavior, your thoughts, and the way you feel, you've finally given it that second thought.

Until you reach this point in your life, you never truly understand the motives behind your actions. You're simply another conditioned part of a society that wades through the deepest, unkindest waters that lead nowhere near your true passions. The moment you realize that self-development holds the key to a better future is the moment the questions come, one after the other. The truth is that Americans are unhappier than they've been for decades. Indeed, the pandemic has caused a flurry of isolation, stress, anxiety, and depression, but one survey speaks for it all. The University of Chicago (2020) released the results of surveys taken at the beginning of the pandemic.

It turns out that, even at the beginning of this ever-changing, unpredictable world, 50% of Americans were no longer satisfied with their lives. Not only do people feel like they've lost control of their environment; they also feel like their lives aren't worth satisfactory standards anymore. This is partly due to isolation, panic, and stress, but it also includes the need for the adaptation we require to succeed in an evermore complicated world. If you thought it was hard to adapt your behaviors, habits, beliefs, and thoughts before, you're underestimating how far more challenging it is now. Only flexible people will truly succeed.

Flexibility means that you need personal development. You need to start mastering the inner workings of your mind. There are many ways to accomplish changes, but one powerful method people are using to adapt their habits and beliefs in this unprecedented world is through hypnosis. Hypnosis was always a popular method for successful, high-performing executives to develop their personal growth and take charge of the direction of their lives. Some of the most successful leaders seeking optimal performance in their lives were paying up to $1,000 for an hour-long hypnotherapy session (Scipioni, 2019).

If people are investing their savings in hypnosis to improve their minds, strategies, and fulfillment, then something has to be working. With science supporting hypnosis, and the magnitude of the power it allows the practitioner to have over their minds, these people have no problem investing in themselves. After all, the mind is where it all begins. Your mind is the key that unlocks the doors you need to step through. Whether you were striving toward dreams for years, or you want to kick old habits out for good, hypnosis might be your holy grail.

Hypnosis isn't intended to replace traditional therapies in areas where you might need them. It's also not some magic cure for diseases and mental barriers. However, it is certainly a powerful complementary tradition that has evolved over the centuries. Professional hypnotism is curated by laws, and learning how to use self-hypnosis allows you to control your sessions within your own morals and inner laws. Moreover, you gain the full benefits from learning how to use self-hypnosis in a way that can't send your life into the pits. There are some cautions to be aware of, and learning how to hypnotize yourself the right way will prevent any issues.

Self-hypnosis has nothing to do with inducing yourself into a state where you lose control. It's not some form of magic you see on stages. Hypnosis is a genuine method of connecting your minds so that nothing stands between them anymore. It's a way for you to allow the inner child to awaken and choose new conditions. In this book, you'll learn every secret behind hypnosis. You'll know about the three minds, and how the functional relationship between them can work in your favor. You'll find answers to why you feel the way you do. You'll understand why you think the way you do as well.

You'll even learn about the reasons why you behave as you do, and how you can use hypnosis to prevent environmental hypnosis. The world is constantly programming your mind in subliminal ways, and this has a lot of influence on the way you behave. It also controls the way you see yourself; it can even change the way you trust and respect yourself. There's so much information flowing around your mind that you can't think straight anymore.

Habitual behaviors and decisions simply become the easier route because they offer familiarity, even if your behavior saddens you. Fear is another behavioral response, and before you realize it, you're succumbing to anxious thoughts and decisions. This will all change by the time you have the tricks in this book under your belt. You'll know where hypnosis comes from, who the main faces are who changed the way we control our minds, and what role science has in this correlative healing technique. Hypnosis is capable of changing the mental and physical ways our brains function with neuroplasticity; the details aren't nearly as complicated as you think.

Once you dive into the art of self-hypnosis, you'll learn how to make suggestions that stick to your long-term memory. You'll have ways to optimize your suggestions and identify the stages through which you may allow your mind to fold. You'll know what inductions are, and how you can induce a deeper state of mind within minutes. Moreover, you'll also know which techniques can complement hypnosis to multiply your personal growth. You'll be talking yourself into a better mood, and you'll use a simple exercise to view various perspectives of the same challenge. You can only change what you can see.

You'll learn how to set goals that fall into the deeper mind as well as use the law of attraction to manifest your desires. There are also lifestyle changes you can throw into the mix to morph yourself into someone you never imagined. These lifestyle changes will be simple enough to insert them into your daily routine, and you'll see mental, emotional, and physical benefits. Part of personal growth is also to seek peak physical health. You can't wish your chronic conditions away, but you can use hypnosis and simple lifestyle changes to manage them better.

The bottom line is that you'll start investing in your growth. Every type of growth requires nourishment and input, or it would simply wither away. You can't confess that you want to master your mind if you're prepared to let it fall apart. The final golden nugget you'll add to your toolbelt is the art of dream analysis. Dream therapy has been used for a long time because it offers us a window into the part of ourselves where our true desires exist. It also gives us the ability to trash any unwanted desires with a method you can't imagine; if only you knew sooner that dreams could be controlled.

These promises may seem empty to doubtful readers and listeners, but I assure you that I've used self-hypnosis to expand my personal development in ways I could only dream about. I'm also a licensed hypnotherapist who graduated from The Hypnosis Motivation Institute (HMI) in California in 2020. It hasn't always been an easy journey because nothing worthwhile comes to us on a silver platter. Everything you feel passionate about and everything you're prepared to fight for requires some effort from your end. I had no direction in my life. I felt as lost as the next person, and my career, personal life, and stability were wading through dangerously deep waters. They would eventually drown if I didn't change something.

For years, I sought ways to improve myself, grow my potential, and manage my well-being as much as anyone can. I grew a stack of self-help books, and tried many methods (some worked a little and others were a waste of time.) The day I started practicing self-hypnosis was the day I immediately knew how my life would change. Never before have I felt such a sudden shift in my mindset. I knew very little when I started, and I only truly achieved my self-hypnosis after graduation. Failures came and went, but that's because I never understood effective self-hypnosis before graduation.

Moreover, as time passed, I also found techniques that worked for me without fail. I realized I was using the wrong suggestions because there are numerous types. Today, I don't go to sleep without listening to one of my own recordings. That's the beauty of it all. Once you learn the correct ways of hypnotizing yourself, you're able to record your own voice and control every moment of the session. Rest assured, I plan to enable you to record your own sessions before this book is done. I've even added 13 sessions to inspire you, and these sessions were carefully designed to help you at the beginning of your journey. As a hypnotherapist, my passion is to help others learn how to control their minds.

The only remaining question is this: How badly do you feel the urge or need to control your mind to be the fullest version of yourself in everything you do and think on a scale of one to 10? If you feel the fire of curiosity fill you up, go forth to learn more about your mind!

Chapter 1:

Three Sections of Mind

The human mind is an exquisite but multifaceted part of us. It has been the center of psychological research, some of which is used to alter and improve certain aspects with hypnotherapy, neuro-linguistic programming, and dream therapy. The mind is fascinating once you learn about the various sections that create a unique person, and understanding these facets can uncomplicate the way you reprogram your mind to work for you. You don't want it working against you. A basic understanding of the human mind can lay the foundation of everything you're about to learn in this book.

Figure Two

Freud's Iceberg

Sigmund Freud was a psychoanalyst who developed the "iceberg theory" that explains the various compartments of the mind (Cherry & Gans, 2020). After analyzing personalities and how they shape our behavior, Freud created the "iceberg concept." His theory, which still influences various types of psychologies today, was that the mind has three main components. The tip of the iceberg protruding from the ocean of our minds is what we call the conscious mind, and this part of your mind is where awareness thrives. Beneath the water lies the preconscious and subconscious minds. These layers are beyond our awareness. The three minds each have a responsibility.

The conscious mind holds our working memory, emotions, desires, and thoughts within our awareness at any given time. Working memory is short-term, and it's a collection of memory fragments surfaced from the other two minds. The conscious mind is where we mentally process information rationally, but it's influenced by the underlying minds.

The preconscious mind is the critical part of the trio. It's where the information lies that could quickly be surfaced into the conscious mind. The critical mind relies on information from both minds as it lies between them, acting as a guard. It protects the conscious mind from information that causes pain or suffering, and it filters the information from the conscious to the subconscious mind. The critical mind decides what goes into the subconscious and what comes out of the long-term memories. This part of the mind works with cognitive bias, previous associations, and cognitive distortions. That's why it's called the critical mind; it filters everything that travels either way.

The subconscious mind is the most primitive part of the brain. Believe it or not, the primitive mind controls and maintains 95% of thoughts, feelings, memories, perceptions, beliefs, and influence (Young, 2018). The majority of your memories are stored in this section, and this can be a problem because this layer remains primitive. It depends on goals, of which the main one is to protect and preserve you. The subconscious has no connection to the outside world other than the information filtered through your critical mind; you aren't normally aware of what it stores in long-term memory.

The desire to protect you can even cause the subconscious mind to influence your other minds because the memories associated with certain informational cues from the senses are too painful, unpleasant, or stressful. The subconscious mind represses feelings and memories deep within your brain. It uses shame, guilt, and procrastination cues to stop you from proceeding with something. What complicates it more is that the critical mind determines what the primitive mind can send into our conscious awareness.

The critical mind is much like a mental waiting room, allowing memories, thoughts, and feelings to be available to the conscious mind. However, the extent of your stored information lies in the subconscious mind. The primitive mind is ultimately the base of most of your behaviors, decisions, motives, and reactions. When you think primitive, what comes to mind? Primitive humans had very little to process other than survival and copulation desires. They had to eat and hunt to survive, and they had to socialize in communities to copulate. Indeed, your libido is as primitive as cavemen. These are two main motives from the subconscious mind. However, the critical mind filters the output; otherwise, you'll be expressing your impulses at inappropriate times.

A "Freudian slip" is a common way of recognizing the primitive mind overpowering the critical mind. You can't say you've never had a slip of the tongue. We consciously intend to say one thing, and suddenly, we allow our ex-partner's name to slip out instead. Another way the subconscious mind pushes past the critical mind is through dreams, and that's how dream analysis came about. Dream analysis can help you uncover repressed memories. Even though the subconscious mind has evolved since 50 million years ago, it still has some primitive tendencies, which love sneaking out before we become aware of them.

Ultimately, the subconscious mind is a mental bank, which you use to invest memories and associations. It's where the source of all goals and motivation lies. The conscious mind has also evolved over the last 50,000 years, just as the world has. It's where logic, decision-making, analyzing, and reasoning happens. However, the critical guard between the two minds is the mediator, and it can be resistant. Now you understand the role of the three sections of mind, but it goes deeper than this.

Working Relationship

The subconscious mind stores information by using the input from the senses, which is regulated by the preconscious guard in the middle. Your subconscious mind is constantly collecting information from the senses, including smell, sight, sound, taste, and touch. Let's say you're about to cross a road. Before you know it (and before you can become aware of it), the critical mind feeds the cues down to the subconscious mind. This happens at speeds you can't imagine, and the subconscious mind determines that the situation is dangerous by accessing the desires and memories stored within it. The critical mind then feeds the given information back to the conscious mind, and voila, you decide to look both ways because you logically perceive danger now.

You won't even think about the dangers before you react to the potential for them. The information that runs back and forth through the critical mind is what we call 'associations.' The critical mind associates crossing a road with danger, and the conscious mind associates danger with a defensive response, such as looking both ways first. The subconscious mind will also associate certain feelings and thoughts for future reference when you need to cross a road again. The primitive mind is what ultimately chooses your state of mind in a given situation so that you can respond accordingly.

The subconscious mind is also divided into two physical aspects, which allows scientists to measure the functionality of it in the case of the stress response. The autonomic nervous system is part of the primitive mind, and it activates before making a decision (Harvard Health

Publishing, 2018). The subconscious mind works on automation, and that's why it's in charge of the autonomic nervous system. The two mechanisms of the autonomic nervous system are much like red and green lights at a traffic light. The first mechanism is called the sympathetic nervous system, and the second one is called the parasympathetic nervous system. Every time an association is required between the minds, the subconscious mind activates the appropriate mechanism to enable the body to respond appropriately.

Both mechanisms rely heavily on the memories stored within the primitive mind, too, so we use 'appropriately' as a loose term. The sympathetic nervous system is the reactive mechanism that switches your body and mind to defense mode, more commonly known as the "fight, flight, or freeze response." The cerebral cortex part of your brain that processes sensory data from your eyes and ears speaks to the emotional part of your brain called the amygdala, which switches on the alarm bells and nudges the hypothalamus to make changes in the body. The hypothalamus gland is like a symphony conductor. It instructs other glands to release chemicals in your bloodstream, such as cortisol and adrenaline, which prepare your body for fighting, fleeing, or freezing like a deer in headlights.

Moreover, the hypothalamus is what switches the sympathetic nervous system on, and these nerves run through your spinal cord to every organ and muscle in your body. Suddenly, you gain strength, a rapid heart rate to pump more oxygen to the muscles and brain, and your blood pressure rises. Nerves are used to communicate between various organs, cells, and glands. The subconscious mind has perceived danger, flipping the traffic light to green, and the body shifts to a defensive mode. The ultimate goal to survive and preserve are the motivations behind this reaction. Your senses also sharpen during this response. The three responses you might experience look like this.

The fight response is when you perceive danger, but you believe you can fight your way through it. For example, a project at work is perceived as dangerous to your homeostasis, which is the balance of things remaining consistent in your body and mind's ecosystem. Indeed, anything that threatens the body's balance with change is perceived as a threat by the subconscious mind. However, you can fight in this scenario by being energized with the stress response to deliver a better project.

The flight response might be experienced when you see a car coming at 100 mph, so you jump back onto the sidewalk. You're technically fleeing from a threat. You're also fleeing from perceived danger when you see someone shady walking toward you at night, so you turn a corner to avoid passing them.

The freeze response is experienced when we feel doubtful or hesitant to proceed in a situation. Perhaps your boss asks you how you feel about the new dynamics in the office. You have no associations stored for this, so you tend to freeze because the primitive mind doubts that you can answer this appropriately. Keep in mind that the subconscious mind possesses no logic. Another example might be when you bump into someone you were trying to avoid; you're caught off-guard, so you freeze.

The sympathetic nervous system becomes hazardous when it activates too often, for no reason, or because the critical mind is making inaccurate associations. The fight, flight, or freeze response is a physical reaction your subconscious mind activates, and it can be burdensome on your body when it continues to happen. Your associations with doubt, stress, fear, and negative emotions become stronger. Constant physical stress on the body can cause medical issues because our hearts, blood vessels, and muscles were never intended to be in this state of mind for prolonged periods. However, this is where the parasympathetic nervous system comes into play, which is also called the "relaxation response" where your body returns to normal functions.

The subconscious mind also relies on sensory information filtered through the critical mind to switch back to the relaxation response. The relaxation response is what makes breathing techniques so valuable. By simply taking a long and even breath in for three seconds and pushing it out gently for six, you can deactivate the sympathetic nervous system and benefit from the parasympathetic nervous system. Either way, the subconscious mind responds with one of the two mechanisms. It creates a state of mind, which is a response. The body isn't the only part of you that floods with chemicals when you activate the sympathetic nervous system. It's the mind that hurts, too. Deep breathing, soothing or familiar words, and visualizing images behind closed eyes can switch you back to a calmer state.

Most people have no conscious control over which response happens, but any perceived threat can lead to one of the three defensive reactions or a relaxed state of mind. Even a single bit of information from the senses can activate either mechanism. You can feel a calming wave overcome you when you hear a familiar and welcoming voice. You also feel at your calmest when you smell something that makes you think of your granny's famous pie. Remember that a relaxed state of mind is also a familiar and calming memory in your subconscious, but you need to absorb the correct sensory information to remind it how great tranquility and relaxation feel.

Hypnotic Control

Hypnotherapy is based on the three sections of the mind and the responses that shape our behavior. Being aware of the state of mind your subconscious initiates is already a great leap toward using hypnosis to grow and improve your life. The subconscious mind is more easily swayed when it has some form of familiarity with older associations. However, it can also form new associations with a conscious effort to insert new data from the senses. Hypnosis allows you to synchronize all three minds so that you have greater control over your responses, whether the incoming information is words, pictures, or the smell that makes you tingle. Hypnosis is a way for you to speak directly to the subconscious mind and make suggestions.

Using new associations, you can trick the critical mind into allowing the subconscious to store new information. One example might be to change your eating habits by slowly associating bright colors, exciting smells, and incredible tastes with healthier foods. You currently perceive healthy foods as boring and tasteless, but by creating a sensory ocean of information for the minds to connect vibrant colors and smells to healthier food, your perception of good food changes with time. Suggestions are words, tonality (and sometimes), visualizations we use in hypnosis to install new associations in your mind. Words are auditory stimuli, and hypnosis uses this sensory information to lay new connections through the critical mind.

If you could change the basis of your being, it would be by convincing the subconscious mind that other perceptions exist. It associates smoking with calming effects right now, but creating the associations to better living with suggestions can change your subconscious mind. You can change negative associations about your self-esteem, confidence, and efficacy with suggestions. Learning how to use hypnosis for maximum benefits helps you prevent the critical mind from resisting the changes. Many people require all five senses to create new associations, but a few people predominantly use one of the three major suggestive senses. They are auditory, visual, and kinesthetic.

Someone who prefers auditory suggestions will focus more on sounds that associate with experiences. These people find great motivation by listening to public speakers, self-help audiobooks, and verbal instructions. They might also be influenced by someone's voice or tonality. For example, you might fall head over heels for someone you've only spoken to over the phone for the last few weeks.

Then, we have the visually suggestive types of people, who rely mostly on what they see. They find it easy to close their eyes and visualize a goal they desire, and their motivation will slowly increase to reach it. Visual suggestions are amplified by colors, shapes, movement, and shades. These people tend to be intensively concerned about appearance, but it's the attractiveness of what they see that makes them desire it.

Finally, the kinesthetic suggestive types of people are those who love feeling the texture of something between their fingers. They rely on physical embraces to connect deeper with people, and they can motivate themselves by focusing on the emotional part of an experience. They feel a deep connection to anyone that makes them feel good.

Whether you rely on a collection of suggestion types with your five senses, or you transpire from one suggestion type, hypnosis is about installing new associations with precise information intake so that the critical mind doesn't prevent it. It's about making your subconscious mind believe and accept new things to be true.

Chapter 2:

Knowns and Unknowns

The associations forming our behavior are habitual, and they stem from lifelong conditioning. Hypnosis is not a new concept because it already happens every minute of the day. Unless you become aware of what influences the three minds, you'll always be stuck in this familiar but stagnant place. Sometimes, the knowns aren't what we want or need in life. They hold us back from our true potential, and they prevent us from trying something new. To be fully aware of the changes you can make, you must learn about the sources of the resistance in your mind.

Figure Three

Psychosocial Conditioning

Many of the decisions we make are rooted in our self-beliefs, which are largely designed in the former part of our lives. We are being conditioned long before we can make logical decisions, and we can adopt negative self-beliefs, depending on the influence around us. An unknown is a situation that requires a response or decision, but your critical mind doesn't know how to associate the other minds, so your response might be to fight, flee, or freeze. Your response might also be far from rational, or you might respond with calmness when you need a little spring in your step. The critical mind becomes confused when unknowns are faced, and this only confuses the other minds. A confused mind cannot decide what needs to be done. Nonetheless, self-beliefs are known associations that come from our earliest days.

A known is an association with which the mind is familiar. It begins as early as childhood. A toddler knows that throwing his cereal all over the floor comes with a reprimand or timeout, so his mind associates the situation with negative outcomes, which might make him doubtful if you're a lucky parent. He will also automatically feel ashamed after doing it because he remembers that it isn't the right thing to do. Take a preschooler who must decide what she wants to wear today. Her mind quickly associates dressing to her mom taking control, making her feel incapable, so she resists choosing her favorite dress. She believes that her mom can choose the best dress for her, and she doesn't believe in her ability to do it. Irrespective of whether the decision involves positive or negative associations, a child already has known associations in their subconscious mind.

A known is anything that stimulates a physical, mental, and emotional response from you. It can make you feel guilty, ashamed, anxious, or excited. Emotions are ways the subconscious mind responds, too. Remember that responses are activated by sensory input, so a child can even see the color green and associate it with the park. Every sense we experience during childhood creates associations to known responses. It's conditioning our minds from day one. Freud focused mainly on the psychology of the minds and internal behavioral influences, but this was later changed into a psychosocial model to include the way the environment plays a role in the development of beliefs, habits, and associations. Psychologist Erik Erickson took Freud's model and developed the eight stages of psychosocial development (Cherry, 2020).

The first stage of development happens between birth and two years. Infants face the developmental conflict between trust and mistrust. Whether a child develops trust is determined by how dependable their parents are. Infants are dependent on food, nurturing, warmth, and love, and poor parenting leads to children who don't trust adults. Mistrust designs beliefs that the world is unpredictable and inconsistent. A child becomes hopeful if the parents cater to the dependency infants need. Even emotional rejection causes mistrust.

The second stage happens between two and 3 years old. Children either learn autonomy or shame and doubt. Toddlers start seeking independence at this age because they need to distinguish between what they can and can't do. Toddlers learn autonomy if their parents allow them to make decisions, choose between options, and potty train. They gain a sense of control over their environment. Shaming a child for making a mess outside the potty can also increase their innate feelings of shame. Not giving a child options can also make them doubt themselves, like the girl who couldn't choose her dress. This is the stage at which willpower develops.

The third stage happens between three and 5 years old. Believe it or not, this is when kids start looking for a purpose. They either develop initiative or guilt. Preschoolers start asserting more control and leadership, but without having the freedom to do so, they can grow into self-doubters who feel guilty about taking control. Preschoolers must have control over the environment to develop initiative, and their keen desire for exploration enhances it.

The fourth stage happens between six and 11 years old. Confidence is often asserted at this age and kids either feel productive and valued, or they feel inferior compared to others. Kids will either be encouraged to face their academic challenges and become competent, or they'll feel inferior because they aren't proud of their progress. Children in a supportive and encouraging environment will believe that their skills are good enough, which boosts confidence.

The fifth stage happens between 12 and 18 years old. Adolescents either develop an identity and learn to know themselves, or they'll be confused about their direction in life. They want to know what their role is, and the environment can alter their idea of who they are. An identity is made of beliefs, habits, and morals that shape the way we make decisions. It's who we are and it guides our behavior. Adolescents are vastly influenced by society as a whole, and not just their friends and family. Not knowing who you are and what your role in the community is can cause painful confusion and a poor self-image.

The sixth stage happens between 19 and 40, and we either become isolated and withdrawn from society, or we become intimate and integrated into the community. This stage is all about finding love and social purpose. It's about feeling like we belong with someone. We want to know that someone can feel the same way about us as we do about them. We want to appreciate and be appreciated. We need meaningful and intimate relationships to thrive in this stage of development. The failure to establish meaningful connections leaves us isolated, lonely, and feeling unworthy. Every stage builds upon the previous stages, too. We believe that we have no purpose, and we degrade our self-confidence with shame, guilt, and unworthiness. Developing this stage with strong relationships leaves us feeling loved, appreciated, and like we belong.

The seventh stage happens between 40 and 65. Middle age people either develop a desire for generativity or stagnation, meaning they either want to generate a better life or they want to remain in a complacent state. People who create things that will outlive them are "generative growers," and people who don't care about the legacy that follows are complacent. Caring about your career and family, and having a sense of usefulness and accomplishment encourages growth. Having low self-esteem and not pursuing greater things to feel accomplished makes you complacent. Being in an environment that encourages complacency can also keep you there.

The final stage happens after the age of 65. This is when you develop integrity or despair. You tend to reflect on your life a lot, and it can either encourage despondency or honor and wisdom. You'll face a crossroads where you need to determine whether your life was meaningful and satisfactory, or whether it was filled with regrets. Reflecting on a regretful life develops resentment and disappointment. You'll feel bitter about all the missed opportunities. However, reflecting on a life well-lived would make you feel wiser, fulfilled, and content.

It's not only what you experience in your three minds that determines your direction and well-being; it's also your environment that influences your journey, and it never ends. The psychosocial part of your development continues throughout life. Your self-beliefs and habits store themselves in the primitive mind up to the age of eight, and this starts slowing down by age 10 (Costa & Kallick, 2019). The brain doesn't require the critical and conscious minds until later because babies rely mostly on reactive responses and primitive goals. It's only once the pruning starts in the mind that the conscious and critical minds develop. Known associations form between a response and stimuli, which creates habits.

Every child is born with more neurons or brain cells than adults, but after strengthening the associations between certain stimuli and responses, the brain starts pruning the excess cells. Often called 'neurogenesis,' the connections or synapses between specific cells grow stronger. It becomes habitual for the critical and subconscious minds to respond to stimuli when you continue to stimulate your mind with known associations. The brain then slows down the absorption of other information to the subconscious stores, and you have habits and self-beliefs for the remainder of your life. These self-beliefs will be rooted in guilt, anger, shame, mistrust, doubt, and a lack of self-confidence. Suddenly, your life script is complete.

Your three minds will refer back to this script whenever you need to make decisions. You'll doubt yourself and question your abilities. Life scripts are often designed with responses we stored to parental and environmental cues. Our habits and beliefs are the root causes of our behaviors, and they express themselves in our self-esteem, responses, and emotions. Your self-image about your abilities, appearance, and personality will change. You go to autopilot behavior where you don't even need to think about your responses and decisions. You've learned how to respond to the association, and your subconscious mind pulls the strings.

Autopilot behavior is behavioral habits. You can only switch autopilot off if you're consciously aware of the habits you continue to enforce. Sadly, we had no control during the early stages, but we have it now. We can change the known associations so that we can improve and develop better habits. Every stage builds upon another, but we can correct the primitive stages with hypnosis because it suggests new beliefs directly to the primitive mind. You can change your self-image from "I'm not good enough, not smart enough, and I'm undeserving of success" by reinforcing positive suggestions. We must change from environmental hypnosis to voluntary hypnosis.

Environmental Hypnosis

Environmental hypnosis refers to everything influencing you every day, including your parents, relatives, partners, children, the media, and even yourself. You can convince yourself that you're unworthy, which happens in your internal environment between the minds. Self-talk is a powerful influence on how you perceive your world, abilities, and self. Remember that the primitive mind has no connection to the external world, and it can't determine whether you're being honest when you call yourself stupid. It also has no reasoning to filter truth from untruth. Every time you tell yourself you're not good enough, internally in the mind or verbally to process the information through your senses, you're reaffirming a negative self-belief. The primitive mind makes this information a known association because unknown associations are unpleasant. Now, you're stuck with a habitual behavior of degrading yourself, and your self-image plummets.

Negative self-talk becomes your truth if you repeat it. The subconscious mind prefers repetition so that new connections form between two neurons. The words we hear also play our minds like a violin. The media is famous for being an environmental hypnotic suggestion. Every word has a specific vibration and meaning to us. Even the tone of how someone speaks can alter our perceptions and make us feel different. For example, "deep sleep" words are associated with sleepy states of mind. A hypnotherapist can use them to convince the brain to enter slower waves. Your subconscious mind is unique from everyone else's though, depending on your experience during the early stages of life; so, different words can induce different meanings to you. You might feel calm when hearing the word if your mother soothed you with it, but you won't feel calm if your mother yelled, "Calm the heck down!"

The media, especially social media, has a huge role in the way we perceive life and ourselves. How can you feel confident if you're watching various fake profiles? How can you feel better about your appearance if the media shows certain body types to be the best? How can you avoid all the bad foods when every ad break promotes candy, cake, and processed junk? These are a constant stream of sensory cues from the environment. Everything you're exposed to internally and externally can write your life script and create autopilot behaviors. Marketing campaigns are the worst because they use subliminal messaging, which is artistry designed around the formation of desires in the subconscious mind.

Environmental hypnosis, which happens every moment of every day, can control your life script, or you can control it with positive suggestions that alter the self-beliefs and habits you want to change. You're being overexposed to stimuli that harm your life, worth, and well-being. Eventually we hit the 40s and 50s, only to question how the heck we got there. We don't even remember the journey because this is what environmental hypnosis does. It's the same reason you lose track of time and miss your exit from the interstate; your mind is being consumed by constant hypnotic suggestions from the environment. You can either be a slave to the environment, or you can set yourself free with positive suggestions and controlled hypnosis. You're aware of where your self-beliefs came from, such as shame and doubt, but now you can exchange them for new beliefs.

The purpose of hypnosis is to change what has been seeded in the mind, especially when you don't consciously desire these beliefs. It takes discipline and practice though. Your current conditioning didn't script overnight, so a new life script won't pop up in a flash either. First, remember that the subconscious mind prefers repetition, and the brain will automatically prune unused habits. Second, a study by University College London exposed the lie about habits taking 21 days to change (Lally et al., 2009). After 96 participants took part in the habit change experiment, it was found that it takes an average of 66 days to break an old habit and replace it with a new one. Use the 21-90 rule in which you practice the new habit daily for 21 days. This allows the unknown to become known before removing the old habits over 90 days.

Otherwise, the critical mind reverts to old habits if you aren't caring for the 90 days that follow. The law of repetition must be followed, and you must avoid environmental hypnosis as much as possible. Take baby steps, and don't overwhelm the critical mind, either. Instead, introduce small habit changes at first. Keep it simple, and use momentum to achieve larger changes as your mind gets used to new habits and self-beliefs. Don't dive into the hard changes first. This only denies you motivation and leads to disappointment. Rewards for your progress also help the mind establish new habits. You need to recognize your progress and encourage more motivation by doing something you love if you've stuck to a new habit for a week or month. You decide.

Chapter 3:

Why Hypnosis?

What makes hypnotherapy a valuable tool? To answer this, we need to delve into the details of how it came about. It started long before Freud studied the partitions of the mind or before the mind was properly understood. However, it quickly gained momentum as the research into hypnosis widened, showing evidence that it could even outrun traditional therapy choices. Hypnosis might be happening all around you every minute, but voluntary hypnosis to change the way your mind works is best achieved by understanding the history and science behind it. Don't worry; it won't get technical beyond understanding, but it will answer the question of why you should use hypnosis.

Figure Four

The History of Hypnosis

Hypnosis has been around as long as the environment has influenced us, but three names stand out. These three names would go down in the history of modern hypnotherapy (Hypnosis Motivation Institute, 2021a).

It all began with Austrian physician Franz Anton Mesmer, who lived in Vienna during the mid-18th century. Mesmer was fascinated by medicinal treatments other than the typical Westernized versions. He believed in astronomy and another popular trend at the time—magnet therapy. It was believed that by placing magnets over sick patients' bodies, the disease could be managed better. Mesmer decided to join the trend and try magnet recovery himself. However, he was surprised to experience a sensation while moving his hands over patients' bodies. Mesmer referred to this sensation as the ability to manipulate a fluid within the body with the movements of his hands. His willpower could change the way the fluid flows. Mesmer realized that everyone has fluid or what we call 'energy' flowing through their bodies, and a blockage of this fluid could be the reason for diseases.

Mesmer's ideas weren't taken too seriously in Vienna, so he moved to Paris in the 1770s, where he gained much support and attention. Mesmer's manipulation of the fluids within patient's bodies was intended to correct whatever was making them feel unwell. Often, music would play in the background, and Mesmer successfully changed the state of mind, which changed the state of being in patients. One patient became hysterical under the treatment, and another patient became cataleptic, which is an induced trance-like state that allowed Mesmer to move the patient's arms and legs under a dead weight. Mesmer's work popularly became known as "animal magnetism" or 'mesmerism,' and it was turning heads. It gained the attention of King

Louis XVI, who ordered scientists to study whether this was a trick or fact.

The next evolution came with James Braid, who tried to prove Mesmer's theory wrong. Born in Scotland, Braid earned his medical degree at the University of Edinburgh. He was a man of reason, but he was intrigued after visiting a theatre where a mesmerist was inducing people into a trance-like state. Famous Charles Lafontaine induced his volunteers into a deepened state of what Braid thought was sleep. They never moved their eyes while Lafontaine inflicted pain with burning candles and electric shocks. Braid realized it had something to do with eye fixation, so he began experimenting on patients and even friends.

Braid dismissed the idea that trance-like states were created by the movement of hands, and he continued to experiment with trance induction by encouraging his patients to fixate their optical attention to mirrors and candle flames. Braid's first theory was eye-fixation and the connection to a sleep-like state, and he coined the name 'neuro-hypnosis,' which was later reduced to 'hypnosis.' Before long, Braid attempted to correct the name because this induction state had nothing to do with sleep. He realized that it sharpened patient's focus to whatever they fixated on, while increasing their sensory allowance. Braid's patients were capable of multiplying their attention to spoken words tenfold, as one example.

Braid attempted renaming hypnosis with 'monoideism,' which means that the tranced patient's attention was fixated enough to reach a state similar to sleep, except it wasn't sleep at all. Unfortunately, Braid's work gained so much attention already that the term 'hypnosis' stuck. Braid was the first physician to establish a scientific foundation for hypnosis, and he named it. His work during the eye-fixation experiments, also known as 'neurypnology' in the mid-19th century, documented 25 cases of major changes in his patients. Braid helped patients who suffered from arthritis, migraines, stroke, skin conditions, and even paralysis. His most profound patient was a 45 year old man who regained some mobility in his upper body after a spinal injury.

Additionally, Braid realized that his patients could control their heart rates and respirations through this tranced state. Braid is often called the founding father of modern hypnosis, and his work established a strong case for hypnosis to be studied further and used in clinical settings.

Milton Erickson is the third man who revolutionized hypnotherapy in the mid-20th century. He graduated from the University of Wisconsin and became the Clinical Director of the Arizona State Hospital by 1948. He was ambitious and resigned to a private practice a year later. Erickson was fascinated with the human brain, and he even consulted the American government during World War II. His work was largely based on the psyche of the Germans and how the propaganda surrounding the war affected people. What many people don't know is that Erickson was dyslexic, tone-deaf, and color-blind during his rise to success. Moreover, he also suffered from polio twice in his life, eventually leaving him wheelchair-bound.

In fact, the American Medical Association even tried to revoke his medical license, but Erickson flourished through the adversities. Erickson's passion for hypnosis started as a personal pursuit to increase his mobility, but he adopted the role of Director of the Psychiatric Research Department at the Wisconsin Hospital in Michigan. It's here that the Ericksonian style of hypnotherapy was born. His experiments began by inducing deafness and color-blindness in patients without sensory disabilities. Erickson's methods were often scrutinized at the time, but they were based on an indirect suggestion to the subconscious mind.

Erickson didn't agree wholeheartedly with Freud, and he knew that indirect suggestions can bypass the conscious and critical minds to reach the subconscious. One of the experiments Erickson is often judged for is when he verbally abused a disabled person who couldn't walk after a stroke. The stroke victim's subconscious mind decided enough was enough, and the man walked out of the room, giving Erickson a huge piece of his mind. Moments earlier, he couldn't even speak. What seemed like cruel and unusual experimentation at the time became what we commonly use today. It's also how our subconscious mind collects data from the environment all the time. We don't need to be consciously aware of what we're absorbing for it to make a difference.

Erickson understood that the subconscious mind often used metaphors and the imagination to create outcomes for storage in memory. He even cured a young boy of bed-wetting by sharing stories of how the muscles work in sports. The subconscious mind saw through the metaphorical stories, gathering the right information to help the boy overcome his unwanted habit. His experiments weren't only based on using aggressive words; they were also based on jokes, riddles, anecdotes, and made-up stories. This is the language the subconscious mind understands. You don't need to tell your subconscious how positive you need to be; you can share stories of how being positive makes you feel.

Erickson also didn't believe in controlling people under hypnosis. The hypnotic suggestion should be voluntary. He would never say, "You will be positive." He would say, "You may be positive if you choose to be." Erickson's work is what most of hypnosis is based on today, and there's nothing cruel about it. He was a unique man, even capable of smuggling suggestions into conversations, but he had morals. Erickson is greatly known for his metaphorical suggestions and the well-known Ericksonian hypnosis style.

These are the three men who truly revolutionized hypnosis, and thank goodness they did considering how much influence the environment has.

Modern Evolution

Our journey through the centuries brings us to the modern era and how hypnosis continues to shape and form our treatment options. Before diving into the connection between the mind and hypnosis, understand that earlier experiments, including Erickson's work, encouraged medical boards to adopt a code of ethics for hypnotherapy (Interpersonal Hypnotherapy, 2018). The laws surrounding the ethical standards of hypnotic treatments were established in 1961, and all 50 states follow ethical standards of their own design. Hypnosis was quickly becoming a valuable alternative treatment, so it had to be structured properly or people's rights would be sabotaged.

Professional code 2809 was established for licensed hypnotherapists, and it included a few guidelines before someone could be licensed. This code states that confidentiality matters as with any other therapy option, and anyone being induced in a professional setting must do so of their own free will. They must also remain in control of their environment and the session so that the hypnotherapist can't make unethical suggestions. Hypnotherapists have to undergo competence training, and they have to remind their patients to seek medical advice from other practitioners, too. The sessions must be recorded and be kept safe.

Hypnotherapists are also not allowed to make suggestions that would go against traditional medical advice. They are not allowed to touch a client in any way, and they may not use their position to exploit anyone in a way that benefits them sexually, financially, or emotionally. In total, there are 20 ethical standards every licensed hypnotherapist must follow. The reason why the reins need to be tightened with clinical hypnotherapy is that it's powerful enough to plant unwanted seeds in the human psyche. Some people would take advantage of this, and that's why many people are turning to self-hypnosis. However, the ethical code prevents issues between the hypnotherapist and the client.

Self-hypnosis is just as powerful with the correct guidance and tips. Either way, hypnosis as an alternative treatment has proven to be 93% more effective over fewer sessions than psychotherapy and behavioral therapy (Cohen, 2019). Now, you understand why science is latching onto the new treatment type. It has proven to be a worthy contender for psychological and physical changes by targeting the subconscious mind.

A review published by Stanford University shares many studies where hypnosis had immensely positive effects on people (Ford, 2015). Hypnosis places the consciousnesses under a microscope and allows us access to make changes. The review covered studies connecting pain management and hypnosis. It also proved that hypnosis is a valuable tool in the fight against anxiety, depression, and stress. Hypnosis even proved to help patients before surgery so their recovery was faster. Select individuals might even be induced deep enough to act as an anesthetic. Other studies linked reduced weight, Parkinson's tremors, and gastric acid production to hypnosis.

One of the main benefits of hypnosis is found in people who successfully quit bad habits, like smoking and drinking. All signs lead to positive results. Of course, some people are resistant to hypnosis, and this makes it a longer journey, but with the right guidance and training, you don't need to be resistant. Science can also explain how these changes happen merely by planting seeds of new perceptions in the brain. In *Contemporary Hypnosis* (Halsband et al., 2009), neuroplasticity and other neural changes were recorded during and after hypnosis to understand how it changes the brain. Neuroplasticity is the brain's incredible ability to transform itself by strengthening specific networks between neurons and pruning the ones that don't belong.

These networks are the connections that allow two neurons to communicate. A thought ignites certain neurons based on memory fragments stored within your associations, and a sensation ignites another network. Every thought, emotion, and sensation ignite unique connections. This is one way of measuring the minds by mapping physical brain activity during cognitive processing. It isn't necessary to consciously process information to light up a network. Remember that most memories are stored in the subconscious mind. Electroencephalography and functional magnetic resonance imaging were used to scan the brain in the above study.

The most profound changes were prevalent in deep hypnosis. The first finding was that the brain slowed down to alpha waves, only measuring speeds of electrical activity between eight and 12 hertz, which is the calm state of mind, also activating the parasympathetic nervous system.

The prefrontal region of the brain also lit up, meaning that peak focus was reached on a singular focal point. Furthermore, cerebral activation proved that participants were more capable of learning words, especially higher-imagery words. The anterior cingulate cortex also lit up, and this region controls decision-making, emotional regulation, and impulse control. Finally, the intraparietal sulcus is activated, which is the region responsible for most of your sensory processing.

This study proves that we can enhance our sensory controls to activate the parasympathetic nervous system when we need to, which changes the way our bodies are reacting from the sympathetic nervous system. We gain better control over the switch between the two, and that explains how many physical symptoms can improve. The study also shows that hypnosis is capable of activating memories of which the conscious mind might be unaware. Memories are often repressed in the subconscious mind, especially painful memories. Hypnosis allows the repressed memories and beliefs to surface to the conscious mind so that we become aware of them. This is called desensitization. We become exposed to these repressed thoughts, memories, habits, and beliefs, slowly taking the power away from them so that two things happen.

Painful memories become less painful, and repressed ideas surface so that we start believing we can change. Our entire lives were sensitized by the subconscious repression, but hypnosis can help us face these memories so that we can change and overcome the painful ones. Neuroplasticity proves that the more we expose ourselves to certain stimuli or memories, the more we break the sensitization we suffered from. Environmental hypnosis sensitizes us, and hypnosis desensitizes us. The greatest evidence in the study is that neuroplasticity is possible with hypnosis. This means you can alter habits by practicing hypnosis at home.

There are also two major differences between hypnosis and meditation. First, meditation focuses on mindfulness and being present in the moment, whereas hypnosis is a form of inception to plant new suggestions in the subconscious mind. It creates new associations, beliefs, and habits. Second, hypnosis has the added value of counting yourself out of the trance state so that suggestibility can't be manipulated by your environment. Meditation doesn't count you out or bring your conscious awareness back to end the session. Hypnosis allows you to keep your boundaries and control over what happens after you reach slower brain waves.

You don't want your subconscious mind to be suggestible to uncontrolled or involuntary influence. Indeed, hypnosis happens all the time while you drive and miss an exit, you sing to your favorite song, and you work until time runs away from you. However, we must remain in control to avoid environmental hypnosis. There will always be moments you experience the fight, flight, or freeze response. You can't control the environment, but you can control what feeds your mind. The purpose of this book is for you to regain control. You can control the mind to feel happy instead of sad. You can control your feelings of empowerment over disempowerment. You're only in control when you know how to change your mental state accordingly.

Hypnosis also identifies the cause and triggers of states you don't want to experience. On the other hand, you learn to trigger hypnotic consciousness by listening to music, sitting in nature, and calming yourself down at your whim. You can recharge your mental state to feel better. One key factor many practitioners omit is that the correct state of mind is required before any suggestions are absorbed. The wrong state of mind can lead to unwanted suggestions seeping in. You'll learn more about this soon.

Chapter 4:

How to Use Voluntary Hypnosis

Now that you know how the mind works, how the environment influences your habits and beliefs, and how hypnosis was founded and proven, you can start learning how to hypnotize yourself. Under controlled circumstances where you have no distractions that could influence the subconscious mind, you can set the stage for the beliefs and habits you desire. There are a few different factors you must learn before closing your eyes and listening to a natural sound until you induce a trance state.

Figure Five

Understanding Suggestions

Hypnosis is the practice of inducing a trance-like state before making suggestions to the subconscious mind, but it's not only a matter of words to which you say or listen. Verbal communication is a semantic construct that stimulates the brain to respond emotionally or cognitively. Cognitive stimulation is when the brain must 'think' to determine what comes next. Where trance is the way your brain enters lower waves, suggestions are any form of stimulation you can focus on post-induction. Induction is the deepening of your mental state until you reach the lower waves, which you'll find many options for in the next chapter. Being in the trance state allows the conscious, critical, and subconscious minds to work as one. Nonetheless, suggestions follow as soon as you're in this state, and they can come in many techniques.

Two main types of suggestion delivery are used in hypnosis. The first type is a "direct suggestion," which is when you tell yourself that you want to feel sleepier or you want to feel happier. It's also used when saying, "You are happy," "You can enjoy," and "You feel confident." 'Indirect' or "inferred suggestion delivery" is what Erickson used in the previous chapter. The conscious mind isn't always aware of the precise intentions, but the subconscious mind is listening closely. Indirect suggestions are also called "covert hypnosis," and they're commonly used in neuro-linguistic programming if someone is trying to manipulate you. A simpler use of indirect suggestion is when you visualize your goals to vacation on a tropical island after the trance state is reached. Your subconscious mind latches onto how this experience makes you feel, making it more genuine and allowing your motivation to expand. Another indirect example is when you say, "You may become sleepier if you wish" and "How would you feel if you went deeper?" You aren't giving direct commands, but rather indirect suggestions. The delivery method you can focus on best is the one that will work.

Post-hypnotic suggestions are simply the affirmations you use after hypnosis once you've counted yourself out. Some people believe that it induces a brief hypnotic state again, but other people use post-hypnotic suggestions to anchor themselves back into higher consciousness to close a session. For example, you might say "I'm alert and awake" as you open your eyes. It's much like what you tell yourself for motivation to get out of bed after waking up.

It's also possible to make suggestions without the trance state. "Misdirection of attention" is a common non-trance suggestion. A hypnotist will direct your attention away from the logical mind so that the critical mind also loses its guard. Misdirection is popular in magic tricks. Waking 'hypnosis' also doesn't rely on the trance state but rather the placebo effect. If you believe strongly enough that your papercut doesn't burn, it won't. If you believe long enough that you're confident, you'll become it. Waking 'suggestions' on the other hand, are also void of deeper consciousness, and they err on the side of environmental hypnosis again. Seeing someone yawn convinces you to yawn, even though the critical mind is awake and alert.

However, hypnotic suggestions come in four forms. The verbal suggestion uses sounds and words, the non-verbal suggestion uses gestures and body language, and the intraverbal suggestion uses tonality or tone of voice. Finally, you get extraverbal suggestions, which include the visual and kinesthetic methods. Whatever suggestion you're using is teaching the subconscious mind new lessons, so the method or suggestion type you use is determined by your preferred learning method. Consider whether you learn better through reading, listening, or seeing lessons. What was your preferred method in school? Did you thrive under a teacher who explained the lesson, or did you prefer to read it or look at images that helped you learn better?

You might be someone who learns better through touching, doing, and experiencing. You need to jump into action. Choose your learning style before deciding which suggestions work better for you. Three rules govern suggestions to optimize them.

Rule one is the "law of focused attention." You need to discipline yourself to focus on your chosen intent before making suggestions. Don't hypnotize yourself to change 10 habits at once. Use suggestions that help you move past your fear of heights until you do it without adding additional fears to the same session.

Rule two is the "law of dominant effect." Strong emotions wipe weak ones out, so add an emotional cue to your suggestion. Besides, you'll be more in touch with your emotional depth while in a trance.

Rule three is the "law of reversed effect." The more effort you place on resistance-inducing suggestions, the less likely you'll benefit from them. Don't simply suggest to quit smoking; this is trying too hard. It's better to focus on suggestions that teach the subconscious mind how great you'll feel when you don't light up anymore.

Positive suggestion is also essential in your sessions. Never allow negative words or gestures to disrupt you in the hypnotic state. Your subconscious mind will start growing the seeds you plant, so avoid using words like 'can't,' "not good enough," and 'incapable.' You should instead use power words to strengthen the suggestibility. Power words aren't magical or unknown. They're words you use daily. Look at these examples.

Word one is 'because.' You're listening to me because you intend to relax and because you want to go deeper.

Word two is 'and.' You're following my voice and calming down, and this relaxes you.

Word three is 'as.' As you hear my voice, and as you feel more relaxed, you go deeper.

Word four is 'imagine.' Imagine your toes in the sand because you want comfort, and imagine the sun on your skin.

Word five is 'pretend.' Pretend like you're gently moving the sand around. Pretend like you're about to implode with relaxation.

Other power words are "which means," 'remember,' 'suppose,' 'more,' 'realize,' "find yourself," 'like,' and "sooner or later." These are everyday words you should be adding between your suggestions while you keep them positive. That way, they become autosuggestions, allowing you to associate specific feelings, experiences, memories, and control over your mind, even when you're out of the trance state. Experience the same good vibes you did in your learning session by repeating positive suggestions. Every time you associate feelings again, the subconscious mind stacks these new lessons on top of each other, making it easier to connect with them next time.

These are the basics of hypnotic suggestions; so you see, it isn't as simple as saying a few words. The last thing you need to do is choose positive keywords that align with your intent. Maybe you want to promote self-love, or you might want to boost confidence. Choose the most basic keywords. You can always swap them around, use multiple variations of them in an indirect suggestion, or use a simple word that promotes emotional association. Even the sessions at the end of this book can have alternative keywords once you get used to making your own suggestions. You can simply swap my keywords and power words with your own.

Optimizing Your Session

Clarity on suggestions will help you optimize your sessions already, but a few more tricks can certainly boost your success with hypnosis. Changing your learning behavior requires intent, attention, and action. The most successful suggestions rely on internal motivation, so it helps to start your intent with something you need. Being aware of your needs in life, especially those that threaten your comfort levels or preservation, can help you set intentions and listen to the right sessions. You'll be more successful this way. Focus on the need to feel more confident so that you improve your performance at work. Don't focus on how you want to improve your performance. You want your focus and intent on the core of your goal. No one can magically enhance their performance unless they enhance the factors that contribute to it.

Also, remember to keep your autosuggestion ideas realistic. It doesn't help to listen to sessions to multiply your wealth by winning the lottery. This omits the action part of the goal. Intent leads to attention, which leads to action. You'll also feel resistance when you practice hypnosis. A time will come where it feels like you can't break through, but this is the breaking point. The subconscious mind will resist the changes before it accepts them. At this point, you either make it or break it. Perseverance and consistency will keep pushing you through the resistance from the critical and subconscious minds. Be patient, and allow hypnosis to teach you new self-beliefs. Remember that it takes time to master new habits and beliefs. Breaking through the resistance will come, and you'll finally surpass the limiting beliefs that held you there in the first place. Another underrated factor in self-hypnosis, particularly, is that we tend to enter a trance while in a bad mood.

You need to be in a better state of mind or your session will be fruitless. It will plant seeds you don't want in your habits. You should never make suggestions while you're in a bad mood, no matter what type of suggestion you're using. Your tone of voice might hide truths the conscious mind doesn't hear, but your subconscious mind listens carefully. Listen to an online session or have a recorded session of your voice for use when you can't make suggestions yourself. You don't want to anchor negative emotions and thoughts with your experience. Your state of mind determines how effective your session is, too. It doesn't help you listen to an amazing YouTube session while you're thinking about how terrible your day was. Once again, you're planting bad seeds in the fertile ground of a trance-induced subconscious mind. Don't even record sessions for future use unless you're in a positive and calm state of mind.

You don't want the subconscious mind to learn how to activate the sympathetic nervous system every time you face the same stimuli. Reverting to tonality, the tone of voice used to record sessions, or listening to online sources, matters. Using the wrong tonality can undo every seed you planted. You might even adopt a critical or negative inner voice because it's been anchored that way. According to hypnotherapist Rory Fulcher, hypnotic tonality requires nine considerations to make suggestions successful (Fulcher, 2018). Consider these guidelines when you record your sessions.

You need a slow speed to induce calmness.

You need clear pronunciations to be understood correctly.

You need a vocal intention to match your goal. For example, you need an inspiring intention in your voice if you want to be confident.

Your pitch also needs to be monotone, so don't create downward inflections for questions and upward inflections for commands.

Beware of feeling surprised by your own voice after a recording. Make yourself familiar with your voice first.

You need to breathe and allow your voice to flow naturally.

You must pause in between to add time for digesting each command.

Your volume should reflect a regular conversation.

The recording should exude confidence, or the subconscious mind won't believe it.

Another way to optimize your sessions is to add frequencies that resonate with peace, serenity, and relaxation. Your brain is constantly vibrating at certain frequencies, much like the low hertz levels you learned about in the previous chapter when you reach alpha waves. Theta waves run at even lower frequencies. Nevertheless, one frequency was found to improve healing (Hypnotherapy Center, 2019). If you want to flow with the frequency that came from mathematical understandings of universal vibrations, you go with 432 hertz. This is the same frequency the entire universe vibrates with. Currently, there are over 50 known frequencies that vibrate with us throughout the day, adding to our environmental hypnosis. That's why music and sounds can change your mood. One frequency you must avoid is 440 hertz because it causes stress. Find a frequency of sounds you can use on

YouTube, and add it to your recorded sessions for better suggestiveness.

Another secret I often use to prevent my mind from going into resistance with the fight, flight, or freeze response during hypnosis is to stabilize my blood glucose levels with protein and hydration before the session. Protein and water inhibit carbohydrates, and carbs cause anxiety (Raypole, 2020). So, if you want to experience the best session, you need to drink water and eat something with protein before induction. Ensure your favorable mindset by also imagining a peaceful and happy place before reaching the trance state. You can continue to imagine this place while you make suggestions, too. Be sure to use your senses in your imagination. Smell, taste, and hear everything. See and touch what your imagination allows. Make it as real as this book you're reading.

Additionally, hypnosis requires a count-out once you come back from a trance state. You can either count backward from five to one and follow it with 'alert,' 'awake,' or an anchor word that stops the suggestive mindset. You can count forward as well, or you can count your breaths and tap your knee when you open your eyes. Count-outs are crucial, or you'll be stuck with environmental hypnosis again. You must condition yourself to be awake and aware.

Now, all that's left is to know the basics of how you practice hypnosis. You need to sit in a calm place without disruptions, and you can't lie down. You'll only fall asleep in the hypnotic state while you're lying down. And whatever you do, please do not practice hypnosis while driving. This is dangerous. Instead, ground your feet to the floor and rest your arms on the armrests of a comfortable chair. Remove noises and distractions, and close your eyes while you breathe evenly for a minute. The last step to knowing how to hypnotize yourself is induction. Many people can't simply wish themselves into a trance state. Inductions are the cornerstone of slowing your brain waves down. They're coming in the next chapter.

Chapter 5:

Inductions Techniques and Stages

of Deepening

Self-hypnosis practitioners don't have someone who can trigger induction with a carefully devised sound and motion. We have to learn about the stages of deepening and how we can reach it. Please note that proper induction is a reminder that you need to be away from any distractions that could plant unwanted seeds in your subconscious mind. There are various stages of deepening, and you'll likely reach lighter stages at first. Practice with well-known techniques will help you go deeper, waking the subconscious mind up even more.

Stages of Deepening

Some people are capable of reaching depths of trance that slow the heart rate down to a snail's pace, and others can only achieve a mild trance state. We underestimate the hormonal state of our bodies and how this influences the induction of hypnosis. That's why it remains essential for you to stabilize your mood and even your blood glucose levels. Any hormonal changes can make it harder for you to go deeper. A study published in *Nature* experimented with the love hormone, oxytocin, to see whether it tampers with hypnosis (Marchant, 2013). The susceptibility of people to induce deeper states was highly influenced by whether they had the right genetic receptors for the love hormone. Introverts are more likely to go deeper, and it makes sense if you consider how they can more easily turn their attention inward. Anyway, whether you're introvert or extrovert, there are three stages of deepening in hypnosis, and finding your depth depends on you.

The first stage of depth is called "light trance" or the "hypnoidal state," and it's the most commonly-achieved state. People who reach this state will usually experience up-and-down eye movement. It's slightly deeper than regular relaxation, but you're still suggestible as your focus peaks. In fact, it's the suggestions and delivery mechanisms that make a difference.

The second stage of depth is called 'catalepsy' or 'hypnagogic.' This is an odd state because you reach a stage of catalepsy where the body becomes lame and immovable, but hypnotic phenomena can still occur. Hypnotic phenomena are the responses your body displays toward external stimulation. You might still feel a pin prick as one example. The catalepsy stage lies between alertness and sleep pattern brain waves. You'll be far deeper than the hypnoidal state, and suggestions will work perfectly well in this state. People commonly experience rapid eye movement from side to side in this stage.

This state can even be reached without hypnotic suggestion or induction. It can be seen in people who sleepwalk and hallucinate right after waking up because their dream and waking brain waves are colliding. The only difference with voluntary induction to this state is that you're in control. Your mind opens to suggestibility, but you won't find yourself placing your phone in the fridge as sleepwalkers do. Self-hypnosis allows you to control the cataleptic state. This is a great target state if you're new to self-hypnosis. You'll learn to deepen yourself further with practice, but remember that it depends on your genetic makeup and hormonal states.

The third stage of depth is called 'somnambulism.' Catalepsy deepens, and you'll have little to no control over your limbs and muscles anymore. You'll be able to raise someone's hand in this state, and it will fall without guidance when you let it go. Somnambulism happens when the hypnosis phenomena stop. Your eyes might also roll back into your eyelids. Your mind becomes blank, and your subconscious can optimally be reached and influenced. The critical mind goes to sleep. No thoughts are running through your mind, and you won't even be able to open your eyelids at this stage. In fact, this stage is deep enough to carry out major heart surgery without a reaction from the hypnotized person (Watts, 2021); it's almost another form of anesthesia.

You become dissociated from the current space and time, and you're more suggestible than any other stage. You'll still be in control of your hypnosis if you've recorded or prelistened to a session you're using during this stage. No, you won't be susceptible to barking like a dog if someone finds you in this deep state. You'll transcend above your current being, and you'll be able to plant the suggestive seeds in the deepest parts of your subconscious mind. This is the stage used by Las Vegas stage performers when they find susceptible volunteers. It's rare to reach this depth when you start self-hypnosis, but practice can help you reach it over time, unless you're not genetically designed for it. Fortunately, this stage isn't required to make suggestions, but it's great if you can reach it.

Practice will help you reach deeper states of mind with the upcoming inductions, but the deeper you go, the more susceptible you are to achieve the greatest results.

Induction Techniques

Induction is used to gently take you to a deeper state of mind before you make suggestions for change. Inductions are guided by suggestions. These suggestions also work on an indirect or direct approach, depending on your preferred method of focus. Direct deepening suggestions would be to record yourself saying, "You are going deeper now." Indirect deepening suggestions would be to say, "You may go deeper if you wish" or "You can relax only if you're ready." Indirect inductions don't use direct commands, and it's useful for people who don't want to feel controlled during a session. It gives you a sense of control, which can even be useful while listening to your own recordings.

Anchors play an important role once you've reached your desired state. After inducing the desired state, or before waking up the conscious mind again, you'll use the law of association to anchor a remembrance of the state or achieved emotions installed by your suggestions. The law of contiguity states that we will associate anything close enough in space or time, such as thinking of cream when someone says coffee. The law of frequency states that we learn to associate two things frequently experienced together. The law of similarity states that we'll associate similar ideas to anything we're thinking about, such as thinking about other birthdays because you thought of one. These laws guide the anchors we use in hypnosis, especially when you want to associate specific habits to certain states of mind.

Timing also matters, so you should place an anchor in your recorded session as you reach the peak of your desired state. Some people place anchors right before they fall into the deep state where they will apply suggestions for confidence, self-love, and contentment. Anchors are like bookmarks that allow you to revisit the specific state you induced, which was then followed by suggestions that made you feel great. The emotional state of your mind after listening to positive suggestions is what you want to recall when you stand on a stage before speaking. Let's say that you're struggling with confidence, so your suggestions will be to make you feel more confident.

Right before waking yourself up with a count-out, you'll place an anchor in your session. It might be to rub your index finger and thumb together, tap your index finger on your knee, or make a circle with your thumb and index fingers. You'll hold this anchor for a moment while you suggest that this becomes the shortcut to your current state. Anchors are as simple as that, and now you can rub those two fingers together when you're feeling anxious and need confidence. This anchor will remind you of the state you experienced, including all the suggestions that came before it. The minds must learn to associate new experiences and states with simple anchors for easy retrieval. Association is the only way the subconscious mind learns.

When reverting to induction, remember to count yourself out. End of session suggestions could include words like 'alert' and 'awake.' Sometimes, there's a subconscious delay with the suggestion, so they might not work instantly. If you experience a delay, you can rather use an ending suggestion like, "Your mind is slowly awakening now." And whichever technique you use to induce hypnosis and deepen your state of mind must be reversed the way in which you came. So, if you used a counting technique from one to 10, you need to awaken yourself with reverse counting from 10 to one.

Four simple induction techniques work well with self-hypnosis, and you can use them in your suggestive recordings if you're recording your own sessions.

Staircase Induction

The first technique is called the "staircase method." This method allows you to imagine yourself descending a staircase, and it uses a direct suggestion to double your depth with every step you take. You would close your eyes and pretend to stand on the verge of a staircase as deep as you desire. You can have 10 or 20 flights of stairs, depending on the depth of trance you want to reach. Look at this example of descending the staircase:

As you stand on the verge of the staircase, you feel an urge to descend into a deeper and more peaceful space.

You can imagine the depth of the staircase, or you can place your foot on the first step down.

Sooner or later, you feel a slight sense of relaxation wash over your mind and body as you stare down this staircase.

Take the handrail gently as you descend one step down because you may desire more calmness.

Imagine your foot connecting with the safe space beneath as you descend deeper into this staircase.

Relaxation and calmness increase as you lower your body to meet the step.

You want to go deeper, and you want to feel more relaxed.

You take another step down toward the deeper part of yourself because it calls you nearer.

The deeper you go, the more calmness washes over you.

Every step down takes you deeper into this space because you want to deepen yourself.

Feel your hand connected to the rail as you guide yourself another step deeper.

Every step deepens your journey, and you can go another step when you want to.

Take it slow as the depth is overwhelmingly relaxing.

Do you feel the need to go even deeper?

You're in control, and you can take another step into the deeper peace overtaking you.

Okay, continue deepening your mind with the staircase for as long as you need to in your recordings. Really imagine yourself in this space. Imagine yourself descending to a place that calls for you.

Finger Spreading

The second induction technique is called the "finger spread technique." It's a rapid induction tool you can use before deepening your hypnotic state with the staircase or counting methods. An example of the technique would look like this:

Raise your palm so it meets your eyes.

Take a moment to breathe deeply while you pay attention to the tip of your middle finger.

Keep breathing in and out as you watch the middle finger.

Imagine your fingers are slowly, very slowly, moving apart while you continue to focus on the middle finger.

More and more space exists between your fingers with every breath you exhale.

Keep watching the tip as your breathing flows in and out, which means you're feeling calmer, more relaxed.

Slowly, your hand is now moving closer to your face, or your face is moving closer to your palm.

Keep breathing evenly as the spread fingers come closer and closer, slowly closing the space between your face and palm.

Your eyelids may feel heavier as the hand comes nearer, and you're relaxing deeper now.

Imagine your eyes falling closed as your fingertips touch your nose.

You may feel the urge to fall deeper and deeper as your arm gently moves back down to your side.

This is an induction that can now lead to a deepening technique like counting back from 10 to one. Use suggestions between your counts, such as "Each number takes you deeper into your mind."

Eye fascination

This is the third technique you can add to your recordings, and it's another rapid induction method to use before deepening your state. The point of this technique is to fixate on something like a candle flame or a spot on the wall to create eye fatigue. This will cause the eyes to start blinking until they slowly shut themselves. In a recording, it might sound like this if you use a candle flame:

Imagine your eyes are glued to the flame as you take breaths into your body.

Relax for a moment while you find yourself fascinated by this moving light.

Feel the warmth of the calmness overwhelm you slowly as you watch the flame dancing, ebbing, and flowing.

The flame changes with every second, and you feel a little more relaxed with each dance back and forth.

Notice yourself blinking and how your eyelids grow heavier and heavier with each one.

The blinks are slow and they're taking you deeper and deeper to a calmer state.

Allow your eyes to shut for a while when they get too heavy.

Now, you can follow this up with a further technique if you feel like you still want to reach a deeper state. Every technique can be deepened further if you stack them. You can even tap your finger against your leg while you listen to the recording of your voice reminding you that every tap takes you deeper into this calm space.

Arm Rigidity

This is the most common technique for rapid induction, and it can deepen you enough if you use the right one. Two options apply to this induction. You can either use the weight leverage of your arms to slowly drop them to your sides and create a prolonged deepening, or you can drop them abruptly, pushing yourself into a deeper state more swiftly. It would sound similar to this in a recording:

Stretch your arms in front of you as you face your palms downward.

Hold your arms in place because you feel like using them to send yourself into a deeper place.

Close your eyes as you breathe gently, and keep your arms stretched out in front of you.

Allow yourself to relax into the chair as your arms feel slightly heavier.

Breathe in and out while your arms are slowly gaining more and more weight.

Imagine you have two buckets of water hanging from your wrists now.

Every moment you exhale is filling the buckets with a little more water.

Now, you'll go deeper and deeper as your arms become heavier with each breath.

Follow the calm state your mind wants.

Your mind deserves a rest while your arms carry the weight.

You feel your body sinking deeper and deeper into the chair as the buckets fill.

Allow your mind to guide you to know when the time is ready to release the buckets.

Imagine yourself falling into your deepest, calmest mind as your arms drop back down to your sides.

This is a short sample, but this technique can be prolonged to make you descend into a deeper stage of trance.

Using the right suggestions, deepening states, and inductions sets you up for rapid self-hypnosis. You're well on your way to hypnotizing yourself for your desired benefits.

Chapter 6:

Complementary Techniques

Hypnosis is an incredible habit to apply to your life, but a few other techniques can turn your journey to goals into an experience you desire, whether your goals are to become successful, wealthier, or happier. In most cases, people look for answers because they haven't found meaning or accomplishment in their lives. Using hypnosis will bring you closer to your goals so that you feel accomplished, and adding complementary techniques only multiplies your chances of success. Please note that I am in no way affiliated with any of the people or methods mentioned in this chapter. I've used them as complementary techniques, and they worked in my experience. Let's review brief understandings of each one.

Neuro-Linguistic Programming

One technique proven to work in rewiring the brain and changing habits is "neuro-linguistic programming" or NLP. Research published by private German practitioner Christoph Sollmann (2016), delved into the details of neuro-linguistic programming to determine how effective it was in clinical environments. Neuro-linguistic programming was originally co-developed by David Gordon in the 1970s, and it has evolved into a variety of techniques known as "mind mapping," 'modeling,' and "covert anchoring." You know that habits are now neural patterns designed to ease behavioral responses with familiarity. Neuro-linguistic programming has successfully changed these patterns in Sollmann's research when it came to helping people quit smoking, drinking, and procrastinating.

The foundation of neuro-linguistic programming is that every person has a map in their minds. This map determines how they perceive the world or reality, and it differs from person to person. No two people have the same map, but learning to know the map helps us use language to reprogram the layout and change the neural patterns. Think of your current map as a route to a destination. Covert anchoring is one method to change the route by teaching the mind how to take a different road. This anchoring differs slightly from the deepening state anchors. The point of covert anchoring is to expose yourself to an uncomfortable habit and associate it with unpleasant outcomes or experiences. Let's say you're listening to hypnosis sessions to quit smoking. Covert anchoring will work if you're associating the habit with negative consequences before applying an anchor.

The same neuro-linguistic routine can be applied positively through modeling. You'll also apply anchors to sessions you can listen to daily, and these positive anchors will remind you of certain states of mind so that you can pursue goals with ease. You don't have to focus on the negative if you want to focus on feeling happier instead. Neuro-linguistic programming was designed to teach you how to think, behave, feel, and pursue your goals like a pro. A coach can help you design a strategy from someone successful with anchors in your sessions that remind you of the ways you must think, behave, and feel. By modeling the behavior of successful people, your subconscious mind starts believing the new habits. Your anchors for positive and negative associations will depend on what you hope to achieve, but you can also watch videos on YouTube from Dr. Steve G. Jones to learn more about NLP.

Law of Attraction Journaling

Being able to manifest the goals and dreams you desire is as simple as using the law of attraction combined with hypnotic suggestion through journaling. Spend 20-30 minutes daily with a journal, and record yourself in the future tense. For example, "I'm so grateful that I've successfully created a strong connection to happiness." Indeed, your conscious mind will laugh at you in the beginning, but you need to repeat it tomorrow and the next day. It will take time to manifest what you desire, and it might not look precisely like what you write down, but journaling has always been a great way to make dreams happen. You're fooling your subconscious mind into believing what you write, and the reason you do it for so long every day is that it takes about five minutes to drop into a higher concentration. You'll become entwined with your journal entries, and more so every day. Three secrets make it more genuine to the subconscious mind.

First, go into extreme detail about what you're writing. Don't simply say you feel happy. Rather, take the entire session to record the reasons why you'll feel happy in this future tense, but remember to fool the mind by pretending as though it's already happened. Second, attach emotions to your entries with your senses. You feel happy that you connected with someone new today. Your heart burst open when they embraced you for the first time, and you love the sound of their voice.

The final secret is to pour yourself into every sensory experience of the entry by focusing on how the pen feels in your hands and how calm you feel as you write. Pay attention to how your physical, mental, and emotional aspects work in harmony while you're journaling. The law of attraction is powerful, and it works in journaling, neuro-linguistic programming, and hypnosis if you imagine the future where your dreams exist.

Gestalt Exercise

Gestalt psychology was developed by Willem Wundt (Cherry & Gans, 2019), and it focuses on how we should perceive the world, ourselves, and experiences as a whole rather than broken fragments. The subconscious mind stores fragments of information, but we tend to perceive an experience by seeing the whole image. For example, you won't notice the still images created by an animator, but you'll see the full picture while the images are moving fast enough to create a movie. This also explains why flashing lights can create the perception of a moving image, even if nothing is moving. What humans perceive as an experience is often an illusion of the whole image their minds piece together.

That's why everyone's reality is different, and many people call reality an illusion. Hence, it makes sense to view other perspectives before making a decision. This is how the Gestalt exercise comes into play. We all experience moments where we need to vent or ask for advice, but sometimes, we don't have someone to whom we can turn. Venting allows us to tell our side of the story, and asking for someone else's advice helps us see their perspective or the perception of their whole image. Role-play is handy in the Gestalt exercise. We can pretend to be two people, debating the perceptions from various angles. You're one person, and the other person you're pretending to be is anyone with whom you want to ask questions or have a conversation.

Start the exercise with a calmer state of mind by deepening yourself into the hypnoidal state. Now, pretend like you're debating a perception stuck in your mind. What would someone else say? What do they see differently about the same experience? Can they pinpoint their differences? This exercise takes practice, but it helps to consider other perspectives before making decisions about your dreams or the direction of your life.

Wheel of Life

Some people aren't too sure about what they want in life. It can be a challenge to be specific if you don't know what your journey is supposed to look like. This is where you can use the "wheel of life," also called the "wheel of happiness." Therapists and life coaches help their clients determine what goals they seek by using a wheel where eight funnels meet in the middle. Draw a huge circle on paper, and place eight funnels with the narrowest points meeting in the center. Each funnel represents a different part of your life. You can have funnels for romance, personal development, career, finances, health, your social life, physical environment, and fun and recreation.

Give each funnel a score between one and 10 with 10 filling it up and one being close to the center of the circle. Color each funnel with a different color, and watch your spider web of current life satisfaction take shape. People need all eight aspects in their lives to feel successful, content, and actualized. If you don't know where to start looking for the habits you want to change, or you're unsure about your goals, this wheel shows you which funnels fall too close to the center. You want each funnel to fill up as much as possible, and you can color it further as you increase these aspects of your life. Now, you can start thinking about what could fill these funnels. Your biggest resistance will come from a lack of motivation.

John Assaraf wrote *Innercise: The New Science to Unlock Your Brain's Hidden Power* in 2018, and he understood that the brain needs to be exercised to promote motivation. The subconscious mind is driven by goals that promote motivation, but you need to physically activate motivational chemicals in the frontal part of the brain by practicing reflection and adding values to specific desires. Connecting the mental and emotional parts of your mind in a reflection helps you feel motivated based on the desires within the subconscious mind. You could reflect on your desired dreams by closing your eyes and imagining how it would play out if everything went as planned. Feel the emotions within this reflection in the most intense way you can. You don't need a hypnotic state for this exercise. You simply need to determine how each potential dream (albeit specific and stimulating for the senses), plays out in your mind and tugs at your emotions.

You might realize that the dream needs a little fine-tuning first. Otherwise, you can determine why you want this dream to manifest. Why do you want your social life to improve? Why do you want your career to take off? Why do you need the fun and recreation funnel to fill up? Knowing why you want to achieve a change in habits, lifestyle, or goals will further clarify the motivation needed. Knowing why your goal is what it is provides a purpose behind it, making it subconsciously more desirable. You can combine the emotional reflection and 'why' tactics to find your goals, too. Use a pen and paper to write down the reasons why you feel attracted to the goals, which lie within the way you feel when you imagine them.

Also, make sure that you're attracted to these goals and that they don't belong to someone else. Your mind can't be swayed by other people's dreams. Mental development only comes from what matters deeply to you and what stirs every emotional connection. Think about how you exercise in the gym to improve and enhance your figure and muscles, both of which do not take shape overnight without conditioning. Assaraf's idea of exercising the mind is similar to this. The brain is capable of changing patterns, designing new connections, and learning new behavior with mental exercises, which may include listening to audio suggestions or imagining something with all five of your senses. Innercise allows you to change behaviors and habits by reshaping your brain. You can also find John Assaraf on YouTube if you'd like to learn more about Innercise, and how Assaraf encourages his followers to connect the emotional and mental sides of their brains to dominate their dreams.

Mental Investments

I've briefly mentioned the "mental bank" concept made famous by doctor John Kappas (Hypnosis Motivation Institute, 2021b). Kappas surmised that we invest thoughts, behaviors, habits, feelings, and experiences in a mental bank. Our investments determine our beliefs and responses to future experiences, which can also influence our goals. What we invest matters because it can bring us closer or move us further away from our goals. What many people don't realize is that these investments can be a motivational surge if we treat the subconscious mind like a bank. Banks require ledgers to see what has gone into them and what balance remains. The balance encourages motivation or a lack thereof.

Think about it this way: If you look at your bank statement and see $1,000 extra this month, you're motivated to spend it on something you desire. That's how the mental bank works, too. Imagine your investments are creating a balance of desires towards your goals. Practicing the mental bank concept requires you to place value on everything you want and achieve daily. There are five steps to creating a mental bank ledger to allow the desirable balance to activate your motivation.

First, you have to define your goals. Take notes from the wheel of life, and write down 10 goals. Use your 'why' to determine which goals matter, and close your eyes to reflect on precisely what you want. Don't be vague in your assessment. If you want to increase the financial funnel, be specific about how you'll do this. You could learn to invest in the stock market, or you can take a leap of faith and start a business. If you want to increase your personal growth, you can make it a goal to read 10 personal development books this month. If you want to increase your social life, you can make it a goal to meet with someone from a dating website each week. If you want a better physical environment, determine how big your house will be, whether it's rented or mortgaged, and what area you desire. Allocate specific methods you'll use and time frames so that you know what your investments look like in the next step.

Step two is to place values on each investment experience. Let's compare your investments to money so that it's easier to keep track of them. First, you want to determine how much you're worth per hour. What is the monthly 'investment' amount you'd like to accumulate? Let's go with $10,000 for this exercise. Multiply this by 12 for the months in a year, which comes to $120,000. Now, divide the amount by 720 hours, which comes to roughly $166 per hour. This is what every hour you spend on any of your goals will earn you. You can even make it more real by writing yourself checks every week for the dollars you earned. Stick these checks up on your office wall to motivate you. You earn $166 every time you spend an hour doing any of your specific experiences. Now, write down value events for every goal you noted. Add these value events to a ledger under the categories it promotes. You only earn the 'money' if you spend time with the value event.

Step three is to create a mental bank diary, which allows you to enter each event and its earnings within half an hour before you sleep. You should use a blue pen and cursive writing, according to Kappas. This helps the entries head straight into the subconscious mind. The diary should contain seven columns. Column one is for the date, column two is for the value event you completed, and column three is for the hourly rate you earned. Column four is for the time you spent on the event, so you can give yourself $83 for spending half an hour on it, or you can earn $332 for spending two hours on it. The amount earned goes into the fifth column. The sixth column records the total entries for the day, and the final column records the balance of 'money' you hold in your mental bank now.

Step four is to make it a habit of allocating values to every investment in your mental bank ledger. Continue recording your entries every night, and review them every week to write yourself a check that goes on your wall. You'll be amazed at how quickly your checks accumulate.

The balance in your ledger also continues to increase unless you're actually paying yourself with financial rewards by cashing each check, which you can do if you can afford it.

Step five is to embrace the changes and experience your dreams. Promise yourself that you'll invest in this bank. Don't allow the bank to run dry because it will demotivate you as much as your real bank account if the balance hits zero. The point is that you need to reach your monthly $10,000 target if you want this technique to work. It's easy to lose motivation if you aren't getting 'funds' from the subconscious bank.

If you're interested in learning more about the mental bank concept, you can read *The Mental Bank Ledger* published by John Kappas in 2001.

There are many valuable tools you can add to hypnosis to turn your life into an enjoyable, successful, and healthy journey, but these techniques have worked for me.

Chapter 7:

How to Stop Negative Behavior

Our lifestyles are another factor that changes the way we behave. Our habits reinforce the negative behavior we don't want, and our daily routines can throw a wrench in the works of rewiring our brains to think and behave differently. Consider someone who wants to quit smoking. How hard do you think it becomes if they have a few packets stashed just in case? Hypnosis won't be as effective if we surround ourselves with the wrong encouragement. A few lifestyle tweaks can alter the influence of environmental hypnosis.

Figure Eight

Positive Self-Talk

Who would've thought that talking to yourself is a good thing? From everything you've learned about neuro-linguistic programming and hypnotic suggestions, you can understand why self-talk can be a negative internal influence over your subconscious mind. However, self-talk doesn't wait for us to sit in silence, induce ourselves into a hypnotic state, or reflect on our goals. Self-talk happens every moment of the day. A thought either ignites the critic or the more compassionate and logical internal talker. Your boss asks you to take another project. Immediately, your self-talk starts chatting away. You can either interrupt and control it, or it can be left to design decisions based on the environmental hypnosis you've experienced for years. The inner critic is saying things like, "I can't do this" and "I have no clue why my boss chose me."

Well, for starters, your boss chose you because they believe in you. Your inner critic will rely on self-beliefs, and these aren't always reliable as you know now. Positive self-talk is a precursor to optimism, and positive thinking can push you past your mental inhibitions grounded in beliefs that don't belong in your mind. Using positive self-talk can even encourage you to push forth when you doubt yourself. Positive self-talk can help you change bad habits, develop new ones, and increase your motivation to pursue goals. Moreover, it has health benefits. It can decrease depression, reduce heart disease, and enhance your lifespan (Walden University, 2021). Start recognizing the negative inner critic so that you can stop it when it mumbles to your subconscious mind. You can't change perspective if you don't identify it first.

Become consciously aware of the thoughts in your mind while you're thinking. Do they sound positive? Do they look for an opportunity amidst the fear? Or is your self-talk telling you how worthless and stupid you are? Stop your inner critic before it feeds your mind with endless negative talk, and take a moment to consider rational alternatives. The alternatives can come from similar experiences, ones in which you overcame the challenge ahead. Using tangible examples from your memories amplifies the effectiveness of flipping negative self-talk to optimistic banter. Keep it realistic though. Don't counter the negative critic who says you can't finish a dissertation if you haven't even studied for your degree. Let's look at a few realistic and positive alternative examples:

When the inner critic says, "I can't do this," you can say, "I've done harder things before." It helps to reminisce on a specific challenge of a similar design you overcame in the past.

When the inner critic says, "This is far too complex," you can say, "A change in perspective to view various angles could help me complete my task."

When the inner critic says, "I'm not good enough to date someone like him/her," you can say, "David/Emma complimented my new hairstyle last week."

When the inner critic says, "I'll only fail," you can say, "I can learn something new if it doesn't turn out the way I intend and I can improve my chances next time."

When the inner critic says, "I don't have the money to start a business," you can say, "I can build a business model to present to potential investors."

Keep challenging negative self-talk, and never allow the critic to take control. Negative self-talk is reactive and causes immobility and procrastination, but positive self-talk is encouraging. Besides, remember that the subconscious mind has no logic, so what it says could be ridiculous enough to laugh about. There's nothing wrong with laughing when the negative self-talk makes no sense. You'll notice how little sense it makes as you challenge it more often. Laughter is a good way to boost your positive mood, too. Other than taking control over the voice when it speaks, you should also remember to use your post-hypnotic anchors when you need them. Use positive affirmations in the mornings so that you start every day on a good note. Repetition is not negotiable, either. The subconscious mind requires repetition, so write a few personal affirmations down and repeat them on a loop.

Affirming your positive mindset for the day allows you to fertilize the soil in which you'll plant your suggestions throughout the day. Take back control of your internal and external environment by adopting optimism, and this can only be done by being aware of it. Don't allow autopilot behavior to engulf your days anymore. A good state of mind also allows you to feel more energized and absorbent, which helps you tackle your day with poise and plant seeds of new beginnings even deeper.

Self-Care

Self-love is the most selfless attitude you can possess because you can't share love without having any to give. Self-love is like restoring everything environmental hypnosis took away from you. That way, you'll regain the love and passion you have for goals, people, and experiences. Practicing self-love is key to changing your habits and lifestyle with hypnosis. You'll re-fertilize the soil before planting the seeds. Self-love is when you start focusing on what you need so that unwanted desires belonging to others won't hypnotize your subconscious mind anymore. You'll gain a greater awareness of your thoughts, behaviors, and emotions, and you'll understand what matters more to you. Self-love even allows you to strengthen your mind with simple daily rituals, such as good sleep hygiene. You can't focus on what you need if you aren't sleeping well.

Our basic needs are commonly dismissed when we pursue goals, especially when we want to become more than what we are now. A few nights of missed sleep can't harm me, right? Sleep deprivation can lead to many mental and physical health problems (Harvard Medical School, 2019). A lack of good sleep hygiene can lead to physical problems like diabetes, heart disease, and hypertension, but it can also cause mental imbalances like chronic stress, which keeps the sympathetic nervous system active. Your mind won't latch on to new habits and beliefs if it's too tired to focus or too stressed to relax. What makes sleep deprivation worse is that it can alter your perceptions and judgment, leading to poor decisions.

Proper sleep hygiene is a cornerstone for anyone looking to change their habits with hypnosis. You need to be in control of your parasympathetic nervous system and the relaxation response to master hypnosis, and a lack of sleep won't allow you to take control of it. The mind and body forget how to relax overtime, and you'll find it harder to induce hypnosis. Make sure you're getting enough sleep daily to ensure a better hypnotic effect. You want a bedroom conducive to proper sleep by adding blackout curtains, setting the temperature cooler, and removing noise and sound distractions from your sleeping space. You can add a white noise machine that helps you sleep. The most pivotal sleep hygiene habit to practice daily is to keep your sleep and waking times strictly to a schedule. Better sleep will ensure better changes with your self-hypnosis journey.

What you eat also matters as you've learned about blood glucose levels earlier, but it also causes trouble if it goes too low. Chances are that environmental hypnosis has already played a large role in your blood glucose levels. You've probably suffered from hypoglycemia as a child, which is the sudden plunge of blood glucose in the body. What people don't realize is that a low level of glucose can exaggerate the fight, flight, or freeze response. It can also create fears that never existed before (Fogan, 2016), which will only keep you in the stress response that wreaks havoc on your body and mind. The body requires glucose to convert it to energy, but it can increase the amount of adrenaline in the body if the glucose falls too low. The adrenaline attaches to muscles and tissue to help the body convert fat to energy in the place of glucose. The constant stream of stress hormones can even attach to your brain, creating associations between fear and experiences while your blood glucose is low.

It doesn't matter if you were never afraid of the experience before. The subconscious mind perceives the body in danger, so it activates the stress response. With time, the subconscious mind makes a habit of activating the sympathetic nervous system when you experience the same thing again. Suddenly, you become nervous and hypersensitive to experiences that weren't a problem before. This is particularly hard for children who suffered often from hypoglycemia. Their environmental hypnosis was consistent, meaning that they grew up with those fears and doubts. Eating protein and drinking water before a hypnotic session stabilizes the blood glucose from being too low or high. So, please reconsider the eating lifestyle you choose before becoming a daily hypnosis practitioner. Your state of mind won't be healthy if you're experiencing underlying stress from hormonal imbalances. Get your glucose levels tested frequently, and adopt eating habits that keep it stable.

Being in tune with your authentic self can also promote self-care, so you have the energy you need. Knowing what your priorities are, setting boundaries, and saying 'no' when the environment or the people within it try to change your routines are part of caring for yourself. To encourage your inner self to be true to what it believes and desires, you also need to protect it from unwanted environmental hypnosis. Sometimes, it's as simple as switching Netflix off or keeping your smartphone on silent. Other times, you need to reconsider the people with whom you're surrounded. Do they respect your boundaries? Do they encourage you, or are they trying to reinforce the old habits you're changing? This is your time, and your needs matter.

Another act of self-love is forgiveness. It doesn't matter what your life looks like right now. You can't beat yourself up for every mistake you made before. You can't degrade yourself for not changing sooner. You're here now, aren't you? Forgive yourself, and allow self-judgment to vanish along with the inner critic. You must not judge yourself during hypnosis. Your subconscious mind will have a field day with negative beliefs if you do. You have to start treating yourself better if you want to love yourself.

Creating a safe place for you to visit when you feel a little overwhelmed is another essential part of self-love. We can forget to care for ourselves when we can't escape the craze of modern-day life. We need a place where everything slows down, which is the same place you'll use for hypnosis sessions. Set up a corner in your home, which is away from the hustle and bustle. Your subconscious mind is far too susceptible to influence when you hypnotize yourself. You also want this space to act as your safety zone. It's where you go to diarize your mental bank entries, journal, and structure your goals. Other than having a place to connect with your inner self, you also want to relax your mind and body with regular practices. Have a long hot shower to relax. Exercise while you think about the reason why you chose the goals you did. Record your own relaxation hypnosis sessions, and listen to them daily.

Deep relaxation is required to promote your self-love or self-care rituals. You can also practice breathing techniques daily to calm your mind before hypnosis. You can even practice them for the sake of relaxing when you aren't about to induce hypnosis. Every time you find yourself having two minutes to spare, take a few deep breaths. Focus on your breathing, and follow it down to the bottom of your belly before releasing it slowly. Repeat your inhale and exhale for two minutes to bring clarity and calmness to your mind, and then carry on with whatever is keeping you busy. Imagine yourself drawing breath like it was cooling the warm tension down your throat, and pretend to be whistling silently as the breath exits your mouth.

It will take time and patience before you notice a change in the way you feel daily with self-care rituals. Don't quit on yourself before you make them stick. Take baby steps to allow hypnosis to change the way you think about healthy living as one example, and make small lifestyle changes to meet hypnosis midway. Being in a better state of mind will allow the suggestions to associate in a healthier, safer, and calmer place where you can pursue goals that won't seem as large as before.

Chapter 8:

Dream Therapy

I dreamed about a place amidst a haugh, and it struck my heart with utter awe. Oddly enough, this rhyme makes sense, but not at first. Ironically, our dreams make as much sense as this rhyme before we analyze them. If ever there was a gateway to understanding the complexities and desires residing deep within the subconscious mind, it would be the window that is dreams. Dream therapy is a priceless tool for anyone trying to master a relationship between the conscious and subconscious minds. Before diving into the upcoming hypnotic sessions, dream analysis is the final tool you'll need to understand the subconscious mind and its inner workings.

Figure Nine

Understanding the Gateway

Dreams occur when the conscious mind becomes inactive and the subconscious mind is left to organize, plan, and store information. To us, dreams are the moving images we watch while we sleep, and they can be anything from interesting to bizarre, but dreams are far more significant than simple imagination tricks. In Chapter One, we spoke about Sigmund Freud as the founding father of the three sections of the mind. Freud also recognized that the subconscious mind has responsibilities, and it doesn't sleep when we do. He realized that while the subconscious mind was hard at work, our dreams were being painted with somewhat abstract pictures. Dreams were stories playing in our minds while our consciousness rested. Sometimes, we're lucky enough to remember the dreams, and other times, we might wake up wondering what just happened.

The phenomena of dreams giving us a window into the happenings of our minds led to numerous studies, as psychologists and scientists wanted to understand how the subconscious mind worked. Research led to the realization that there are three dream phases (Laves-Webb, 2020). The first phase is related directly to what happened during the day. The subconscious mind must process the events of the day, whether they were traumatic or blissful. The brain operates at a higher emotional level during sleep, so the first thing it does is process the emotional events of the day. This tends to happen within the first three hours of sleep. The subconscious mind may make associations between certain emotions and events that the conscious mind was too anxious or traumatized to make. Perhaps you would consciously feel ashamed or guilty if you made these connections while awake. Subconscious repression happens during this phase.

The second phase of dreaming occurs around midnight for about two hours. The subconscious mind is practicing for the future based on what it knows during this stage. The amygdala is highly active, and it might even test a few challenges in your subconscious mind before these challenges are faced in waking moments. For example, you may dream of being on a stage, but you're afraid of public speaking. So, the amygdala and subconscious minds experiment with your fearful state, which may or may not be symbolically displayed in a dream; it's almost as though the subconscious mind is exposing you to information to desensitize your reactions. However, this phase of dreaming can also hold the key to future possibilities and opportunities. It might be where you see the deeper desires of the subconscious mind.

The third phase is where the subconscious mind organizes your memories for storage or disposal. This is often called the "venting phase" of dreams. The venting phase allows the brain to determine what needs to be stored in long-term subconscious memory and what can go. This phase happens during the early hours of the morning. The brain digests what happened during the day, what needs to be recalled later, and what needs to be put better into the context of where your life is right now. The venting dreams are a gateway for dream analyzers to rid the body and mind of unwanted or negative thoughts and emotions.

There are a few issues with dream analysis. The subconscious mind makes no sense, so don't expect the stories to resemble any form of logic. You could be dreaming about scaling up the walls, which would indicate that you're trying to escape from something unpleasant. You might dream about being stuck in the backseat of a car rushing down the interstate without a driver. This dream shows that you have no control and you need to take it back. Dream analysis loses its linear shape if you think it will give you a direct message; it won't. The subconscious mind is like a primitive caveman, drawing pictures on your dream walls. Unless you analyze the two factors of each dream, you won't understand it. Indeed, some people are lucky to have straightforward dreams, but most people have dreams that contain 'latent' and 'manifest' content.

Latent aspects are the parts of your dream you can immediately understand. They are the true aspects of the current context of your life. Dreaming about someone you lost might simply indicate how much you miss them. There isn't necessarily a symbolic meaning to it. However, many dreams have a combination of latent and manifest aspects. Manifest aspects are symbolic, such as the car symbolizing control and the wall symbolizing the feeling of being trapped. One simple way to determine whether the content is true or symbolic is by fitting it into the context of your life in the present. When you recall the dream, do you feel as though you understand every aspect of it without much thought? If not, the confusing aspects often represent symbolic meanings.

This is the first stage of "free association." Your conscious mind will freely and quickly associate meaning to true aspects but suffer from confusion with symbolic aspects. Dream analysis might seem complicated, but it's become simpler with so many online resources now, even if you have to translate symbolic dreams. The final challenge with dream analysis is "conscious memory." Ninety-five percent of people forget their dreams within minutes after waking up (Nichols, 2018). The secret is to make sure a dream journal sits on your night stand next to your bed so you can record the dream before it fades. It must be recorded in explicit detail because a single lost symbolic aspect could change the meaning of the entire dream.

Overcoming the few challenges with dream analyses is simple with a diary, online resources, a dream therapist, and knowing the difference between true and symbolic meanings in the context of your life. Something may be symbolic to you, but it might be true to me. Nevertheless, dream therapy allows you to use the subconscious gateway to reinstate memories previously repressed by the primitive, protective mind, and it can help you manifest better results in your goals if you know how to influence your dreams. Dream analysis can even help connect us to the authentic part of ourselves once we expose memories, thoughts, and feelings we weren't aware of before.

It can also help us process negative emotions and self-beliefs more healthily, and we can vent out the unwanted self-beliefs in the early morning hours. We can even use our dreams as a base to find answers to challenging questions in our lives if we target the second phase of sleep. This allows the brain to experiment with new ideas for goals you consciously desire so that it can see whether the ideas will work or not. Dreams are a source of inspiration and insight into the deepest parts of your mind. You simply need to connect with them and remember to write them down in every detail when you wake up or you'll forget them.

How to Analyze Dreams

Understanding what story your dreams are telling you can open your life to new inspiration. A dream therapist can help you translate the symbolic meanings behind your abstract stories, or you can write them down in great detail so you can use online dream dictionaries to understand the potential meanings. Two good online resources are www.dreammoods.com and www.dreamdictionary.org. These resources list symbolic dream aspects in alphabetical order, making it simpler to find what you're trying to interpret. Sometimes, you can also experience recurring dreams that might not even look the same at the time, but you'll notice similarities in meanings when you interpret the symbolism over a few days or weeks. You must keep a dream journal so you can record patterns.

Let's say you dreamed about washing your hands last week, and you followed this with a dream about a judge striking a gavel a few days later. Perhaps this was followed by a dream that contained red hands. When looking at all three dreams, there's one similarity. Washing hands can indicate feeling ashamed or guilty of something. Striking a judge's gavel could indicate judgment, and red hands could indicate blood on your hands. All three dreams lead to the subconscious mind feeling guilty about something. It might even feel shame as well. Now, place these dreams into the context of your current life. Is there any decision you've made recently which might make you feel guilty inside? Perhaps there's a decision you're about to make that you're uncertain of because it might make you feel guilty.

This is where the second stage of free association remains key to understand how symbolic dreams should be interpreted in your unique life. You may connect hand washing to guilt, but I may connect it to a poor relationship I've wanted to end. I'm washing my hands of the person who hurt me. You have to determine what your contextual role in the dream is and how it fits into your current life. Symbolic meanings are often strongest when we allow our intuition to guide our free association. If you read that red hands indicate guilt, and you don't feel like this interprets your situation, then you need to look at other meanings. Your dreams will expose deep emotions and who you are, but dreaming that you're watching the judge's gavel strike doesn't mean you feel guilty. The dream is too vague anyway. Who's the judge? Who's in the courtroom? Where are you?

What other details happened? What colors, shapes, and sounds do you notice? Is the dream happening in the present, future, or past? Use the two-column technique to record your dreams every morning. Divide the right-hand side of each page with a line down the center. Use the left side of the page to write out your dream as best you can remember. Now, write the true aspects of the dream in the left column and the symbolic aspects in the right column. Keep reading your dream essay until you record every detail required in the two columns on the right. Listen to the sounds in the dream. Determine what color the car is before recording the type of car. Name the people if you can, and think of who the unknown people remind you of in your life. If you're not the judge, someone you know might be the judge.

Now, go on to one of the online dream dictionaries, or discuss the week's dreams with a therapist. The therapist is trained to identify symbolic meanings, and they'll try the free association trick with you to see if their interpretations resonate with the context of your life. If they don't, they'll offer you a different meaning to test the associations again. You'll be asked to share the first thoughts that pop into your mind while they read the symbolic aspects in the first stage of free association, to determine whether the aspects are symbolic or not. Then, you'll be asked if their interpretations relate to what is happening now, what happened in the past, and what you're expecting of the future, which is the second stage of free association. If you're interpreting your dreams yourself, you can write down the meaning of each symbolic aspect. Then, you can go through the list and do both stages of the free association assessment on yourself.

Does the interpretation mean anything to you? Does it ignite an automatic thought? If not, look for different meanings of the same symbolic aspects. The symbolic aspects should somehow fit into the true aspects or your life. Look for the fears in your dreams so you can do something about them. Look for the emotions you haven't processed, which you can target in your hypnosis sessions. Watch out for inspiring messages in the middle phase of your dreams because you might learn something new. For example, I'll use one of the most commonly interpreted dream aspects. You're standing at a crossroads, and you see a split on a dirt road. Pay attention to the details around this dream. Is the grass taller on one side of the road? Do you feel anxious about one path and not the other?

Look at the condition of the road, and try to identify details that give away the destinations of each path. Perhaps one path leads up toward a mountain, and the other path leads down into a valley. You might be facing a professional decision about two new careers. The one might be situated on the top floor of a building, and the other one may be situated on the ground floor. Focus on the length of the grass to see which path strikes less fear. Focus on the way you feel when you look at each path. There can never be enough details from your dreams. You might not remember them all, but that's why you'll wake up and grab the pen immediately. You also don't have to interpret the dreams daily. You can do it once a week. This will help you identify dreams with recurring messages, even if the dream landscapes differ.

Using Dreams to Inspire Change

Interpreting dreams isn't as difficult as some people believe. Influencing the dreams to get inspiration or answers from them is another story, but don't worry; it's also not rocket science. Dreams are not only a way to reflect on ourselves, our desires, and our underlying emotional state. They're also a way for us to connect the dots we can't while consciously awake. We can influence our dreams by focusing on a thought or idea five minutes before sleeping. A study in *The Journal of*

Sleep Research confirmed that participants who suppressed intrusive thoughts five minutes before sleeping were overwhelmed by them in symbolic and true aspects in their dreams (Kröner-Borowik et al., 2013). This seems negative, but it only confirms that our thoughts before sleeping are highly influential in our dreams. We can use this advantage to process fears in the second phase of dreams, potentially finding answers; or, we can use it to vent unwanted thoughts and emotions.

Write down what you want to know on a piece of paper before sleeping, and then calm your mind down for five minutes with a deep breathing exercise while you focus intently on the written question. Your mind should be relaxed, similar to hypnosis, but you must focus intently on the question you wrote before nodding off. Having a relaxed mind helps you remember the dreams when you wake up, and you'll record them quickly before starting your day. Your question can be anything you need to answer, and it will come to you in your dreams. It might come in symbolic aspects, but your mind was focused enough on your concern or query before sleep to encourage the subconscious mind to sort through possible answers. You can also use the same exercise to write down thoughts and emotions you want to vent in the morning hours, and maintain your attention on ridding yourself of these unwanted thoughts.

Dream therapy gives you another way of communicating between the conscious and subconscious mind. Never take your dreams for granted. You don't know what they're trying to show you until you interpret them.

Chapter 9:

Hypnosis Scripts

Please note that these sessions are guided strictly by the ethical standards of hypnotherapy. You will not be hypnotized in such a way that you have no control. The sessions will include direct and indirect suggestions, and the depth of your induction will depend on you. You're also welcome to use these sessions as guidance to create your own by replacing suggestions and anchors with those which you feel are most comfortable. The sessions include suggestions to break bad habits, change emotional states, and overcome fears. They are best listened to, but you can also pretend to have a hypnotic tonality if you're reading them. They might not be as effective while reading them, but you can use them to record your sessions then.

The Cravings Eraser

This session is dedicated to someone who wants to dissolve their cravings for sugar, candy, and other unhealthy foods.

Start with making yourself comfortable. Perhaps you want to sit in a chair, or perhaps you'd like to rest your arms on your sides as your eyes slowly fall closed.

Take a long and deep breath, drawing all the air into your body, allowing you to sink a little deeper into the chair.

Every exhale you release will slowly sink you deeper into the chair if you wish.

You might want to take 10 more deep breaths, slowly and steadily.

Press the air out gently as you fall deeper into the comfort of the chair.

Nine deep breaths remain as you draw another one slowly and gently.

You're only eight breaths away from where you want to end in the depth of this relaxation.

Take another breath into your belly as you reach seven now.

Take the sixth breath as your body collapses deeper with the exhale.

Perhaps you want to pause for a moment and recognize how comfortable you're becoming.

If you're ready, continue counting down your deep and even breaths as the chair engulfs you more.

Follow the air in and out as you reach the fourth breath that only sends you even deeper.

You may let go of the part of you that wants to deny this deep comfort.

Draw breath number three deep into your body and feel it circulate through you.

Exhale and fall deeper into the chair as you draw breath number two.

Hold the breath for a moment to allow a deeper fall with the exhale.

You're nearing the deepest parts you want to experience as you draw the longest breath.

Imagine yourself falling into a new depth you've never experienced before as you press the air out gently.

You may feel lighter. You may feel as comfortable as you wish.

There's a beautiful calmness in this new depth.

I want you to rub your index finger gently against your thumb.

Allow the friction between your fingers to assert yourself in this serene space.

You're allowed to release your fingers when you wish now.

You may stay in the serenity of this place.

Allow the calmness to overtake you as you pretend to see a mirror across the room.

Imagine that you're seeing yourself in this reflection.

Pay attention to the wonderful feelings making themselves known throughout your body and mind.

You're more relaxed than you could imagine.

Allow yourself to face the reflection.

Watch every line and curve on your body, and allow these images to consume your mind.

Study the person in the mirror.

There's also something else in this peaceful space that attracts your nose.

A table stands to the right of the mirror.

On this table stands a cake and many other unhealthy treats.

But now, there's another table attracting you to the left of the mirror.

It's okay, you can see what this table offers, too.

Maybe you see healthy vegetables and a scrumptious piece of grilled salmon.

The smell coming from this table is interesting. It's new.

Allow yourself to feel what you want as your attention slowly passes your reflection and goes back to the cake table.

I want you to take a step back now.

Imagine you're stepping back so you can see yourself better in this mirror between the tables.

Your eyes feel fixated on the cake table, but something else catches your eyes.

Your reflection doesn't look so healthy.

Imagine seeing pimples forming on your face.

Imagine seeing your body round out a little.

This reflection makes you feel a little sad and disappointed. It's okay to feel sad about it.

Move your attention back to the healthy table for a moment.

Watch this table as your reflection eventually draws your attention again.

You look more and more healthy with every passing moment.

The pimples are vanishing, and the roundness is leaving your body.

Embrace the good feelings coursing through your mind and body as you watch your reflection take a new form.

Move your attention back to the healthy table, and notice what lies upon it.

The smells of these incredible ingredients are swarming your nose now.

The cake table has disappeared like a light switch was flipped.

Move your focus back to the reflection, and continue to watch it grow healthier in every way.

Allow the emotions of this change to overwhelm you.

You may feel happy. You may feel excited. You may feel like a new person.

It's okay. Spend a moment in this incredible space.

Now, allow yourself to come back slowly from this depth.

On the count of one, you draw another breath.

You may feel yourself moving away from this image.

Count two as you draw another breath and focus on how the image grows more distant.

Count three as you move further away from the deep image.

Count four as you may start feeling yourself back in the chair.

Continue to five as your hands feel like they carry a small weight again.

Count six as you draw another breath into your lungs to open your awareness.

Go on to seven as you take another breath to add more weight to your body in the chair.

Continue with another breath as you reach eight.

Count nine as you feel yourself fully back in the chair now.

And on the count of 10, I want you to wake up fully. I want you to open your eyes and be alert again.

Optimistic Motivation

This brief session helps you become more optimistic and motivated to start a project on which you procrastinated. It can help you burst through the negative resistance. We'll use a rapid induction technique with this one.

Rest your feet against the ground as you sink comfortably into a chair.

I want you to raise your right hand so your palm is a few inches from your face, and your fingers are touching each other.

Take three deep breaths into the core of your body while you focus on the tip of your middle finger.

Take another three deep breaths as the air flows through to the core while you pay attention to the tip of the middle finger.

How deep you fall into this calmness is all in your hands now.

Take another three deep breaths as your eyes fixate on the tip of the middle finger.

You may start noticing the fingers are moving apart now.

You may allow them to continue moving apart slowly.

Maintain your focus on the middle finger as they move further and further apart.

Your hand feels relaxed now, and you can see something new happening.

Your palm is either moving slowly towards your face, or your face is moving closer to your palm.

Continue breathing evenly and focusing on the tip of the finger while it comes closer and closer.

There's no force. It's just happening.

You can feel your eyelids growing heavier as the tip of your focused finger nears your forehead.

And as it touches your forehead, your eyes fall closed.

Your arm slowly makes its way back down to your side where it rests.

Continue breathing in and out slowly as you realize how calm and relaxed you feel.

Your mind has slowly wandered into a deeper space, one where you control how relaxed you feel.

You can hardly feel the chair under your skin anymore as the calmness overcomes you.

Your mind may seem clearer than ever before.

It only becomes more and more clear with every passing moment.

Take a moment to tap your thumb and index fingers together gently to remind you of how you feel at this moment.

Your mind is more open and more focused.

Tap it five times, and then you may release them.

Now, I want you to imagine yourself sitting at your desk.

It might be a desk, or it may be a table.

Pretend to sit in front of a place where you think about work.

It feels different this time. Your mind doesn't feel hesitant.

Instead, your mind is opening up to a new level of clarity.

Imagine a task you've put off for some time now.

Pretend as though this task is on this table in front of you.

This task, project or whatever you wish to complete has been a thorn for you.

You always felt anxious about completing it. You doubted yourself and your mind became resistant.

But, it's different this time because your mind feels at ease. Your mind is paying attention to the details it couldn't see before.

You don't feel the negative resistance present in this imagined state anymore.

Realize how you see the project now. Recognize the way you feel when you look at it with an open, positive mind.

You may even believe in yourself now, and you may believe you can complete it better than anyone else.

Allow yourself to feel motivated as you watch the various aspects of what needs to be done.

Maybe you feel a smile crossing your face as you watch the pieces that need to go together.

Your motivation only grows larger and larger with every positive thought in your mind.

You see yourself taking the first step to completion.

Pretend as though you're working on this project now, and every passing moment doubles your motivation.

The more your motivation grows, the more positive you feel.

You may even feel happiness tingling at your core as you continue taking more and more steps towards completing the project.

Feel the emotions traveling from one end of your body to the other as you complete another step of your project.

Imagine yourself placing the images together while the project takes shape.

It once looked like a puzzle, but now it's coming together to create something beyond your wildest imagination.

Your motivation continues to flourish as your optimism grows with each step toward the end of the project.

You've never felt this surge of positive affect before.

You broke through the barriers that held your mind in a resistant place.

You feel a sense of freedom as unfamiliar as a new language.

The only difference is that you understand every word and instruction standing between you and the completion of your work.

Stay in this new freedom as long as you need to while your mind continues to inspire, transform, and create.

Allow every emotion to wash over your deepest core before you come back.

It's a wonderful place to be, but you can bring this feeling back to your conscious self.

You can draw it like a magnet to the world outside of this space.

Focus on your breathing for a moment again while you slowly come back to the chair.

Your right arm makes its way to your face again as the fingers touch your forehead.

You may allow this to happen as slowly as you need, and remember that the feelings from the imagined space will return with you.

Your fingers are gently moving away from your face now, and your eyes are opening slowly.

Allow yourself some time to refocus on the physical space you possess.

Watch as your hand moves away from your face, allowing you to feel more awake and alert with every inch.

As your fingers move back together, you feel fully alert again, and you can drop your hand to your side now.

Deep Relaxation

This session is to induce deep relaxation, and it helps you to calm yourself before or after a stressful situation. It guides you in a way that switches your parasympathetic nervous system on so you can enjoy the relaxation response you deserve. I'm going to use the Rainbow Mountains in Peru as a peaceful place to relax, but you can change this in your recordings to suit any place that makes you feel relaxed. It might be a vacation spot or a place you've always wanted to visit. Also, feel free to research the Rainbow Mountains before entering this session so you can truly engage with the beauty of it.

I want you to relax into a comfortable seat where you can engulf yourself in every moment of this journey.

There's no need to close your eyes for as long as you can keep them open.

I want you to find one thing you can focus on, whether it's a spot on the wall, a tree in the garden, or a piece of colorful paper you placed on the table in front of you.

Choose a piece of paper with your favorite color, and send all your focus into the circle you cut out.

Take a breath in as you maintain your locked sight on this piece of paper.

It's okay if your focus wanders off a little from time to time. Gently bring it back to the piece of paper.

Pretend as though the circular piece of paper is slowly spinning around, making the color grow brighter and brighter.

Take another calm and relaxed breath as your paper draws your attention like a magnet.

Feel yourself glued to the paper as you double your depth with every passing moment.

Your eyelids feel a tiny bit heavier as you become more and more relaxed.

Allow yourself to fall into the chair beneath you as each breath takes you into a deeper, calmer space.

Imagine the chair wrapping itself around you as you start blinking.

It becomes harder and harder to maintain your focus on the paper while your eyes grow more and more tired.

It's fine. This is a safe space to fall into your deepest relaxation.

Allow the color within the paper to draw you nearer as your eyes become even heavier.

Every blink sends you deeper into the wrapped comfort of the chair.

When you feel like you can't keep your eyes open, allow them to fall shut, sending you down a deeper path to relaxation.

Your breathing becomes more and more even as your muscles feel like they melt into the surface of the chair.

The calmness is absorbing your mind and body. It's overtaking every muscle, one by one.

Before your muscles fall into the deepest depths you wish to achieve, allow your index finger to tap gently against the armrest.

Keep tapping as you experience an even deeper calmness with each tap.

Tap three more times to embed the upcoming journey so deep in your mind that you can't lose it.

Now, you can release the tapping and listen to my guidance. I wish to take you to a special place that exudes relaxation.

I want you to imagine yourself on a vacation in Peru.

Pretend as though you've just departed from the bus on a horse headed to an incredible place.

You can also imagine yourself walking if you aren't too fond of horses.

The walk or ride will gently cradle you into a deeper relaxation until you reach the penultimate place.

This may continue for as long as you wish to feel the calmness and relief.

Imagine the horse moving gently underneath you.

This horse is friendly, and it will only go as fast as you wish.

The tamest and safest creature is moving gently and soothingly beneath you.

Each time this magnificent creature's hoof connects with the ground, the movement rocks you into a deeper relaxation.

Follow the movements of this horse as you make your way down a path.

Allow yourself to move back and forth with every motion of this incredible beast.

Imagine your muscles releasing a little more tension with every step the horse takes.

Feel the connection between yourself and this powerful beast.

The horse may be powerful, but you're in control of its every movement.

Pretend like the horse is an extension of your body as it takes another step, sending you into an even deeper calmness.

You're in charge of how fast the horse travels.

Stay with this horse, allowing each bit of calmness to consume your every fiber of being.

Before long, when you're ready, you may reach the peak of the mountain that overlooks the valley below.

Imagine yourself looking out over this magnificent landscape as you feel more relaxed than you could ever dream about.

The colors flowing through each ebb and curve are intricately beautiful on every level.

Allow these colors, blue, yellow, orange, red, and green, to draw your attention to the curves across each mountain.

Be with yourself in this beautiful place with this horse beneath you, or you can imagine friends and family who make you feel relaxed in this space with you.

Calmness is the only reality as you continue to scan the landscape.

Listen to the gentle breeze at the top of this peak, or listen to the sounds of the soothing voices of people who accompany you on this journey.

Have you ever seen something that touches the deepest parts of your soul like this?

Have you ever truly experienced the glory and beauty of nature in this way?

Spend as much time here as you wish, and feel every ounce of joy flood your body as it sits in comfort on top of this mighty beast.

When you've had enough of this picturesque landscape, you can allow the horse to return.

Pretend as though you're guiding the horse back down the path now.

The movements of this incredible beast are awakening each muscle with every step this time.

Feel the power transfer from the horse to your muscles as you near the end of the path coming back from this beautiful place.

Allow each trot to awaken another muscle.

Before you realize it, the horse is but an imagined creature. You still feel deep calmness in your mind, but the horse has slowly vanished.

Imagine yourself sitting back in the chair now.

Your eyes may open slowly as you count back from three to one.

You take a deep breath as you reach one, and you feel fully awake again.

Sleep Induction

Sometimes, we struggle to sleep, and hypnosis can create the right state of mind to drift off. This session comes with a few warnings though. Please do not listen to it while driving or operating anything that could bring you harm. Also, whether you lie down or sit in a chair will depend on a key factor. This session must not be listened to in a lying position if the following session starts automatically. This creates an overlap of sessions while you're asleep. You may not want to use the session after this without being induced and woken properly. The only time you listen to deep sleep sessions to fall asleep in a horizontal position is when you have a single recording and a guarantee that nothing else can distract your session. Otherwise, you can listen to the session in a seated position until it ends, and then you can lie down to sleep.

You're about to go on a journey to promote a sleepier state if you wish.

You may listen to my voice as I carefully and gently take you deeper.

Every time you hear the word 'deeper,' your busy mind will slow down more and more.

Close your eyes as you listen to my voice, and imagine yourself standing on the verge of a spiral staircase.

The staircase is as long as you need it to be, and the depth of it will expose you to a slower, calmer mind.

Take the handrail to your left, and pretend as though you're about to embrace the downward staircase.

Take a deep breath as you lower your foot to the first step.

You may allow your hand to slide one notch down the rail as you take another step with your other foot now.

The staircase feels warm and welcoming as you continue taking baby steps down the spiral.

Feel how your foot connects to the next step down, and embrace the depth as you go deeper and deeper.

Continue breathing evenly as you take another step towards the end of the first curve.

You may already be feeling a little more tired by now.

That's okay; allow yourself to embrace the subtle changes in your mind as it slows down further and further.

You're about to enter a new curve, and this one is more special than the last one.

Take your right hand and use your index and middle finger to make gentle circles against your leg.

Keep making these circles before you descend deeper into the staircase.

Allow each circle to remind you how you feel at this very moment.

Release your circles and relax your arm again once you're ready to descend into the new curve.

This curve has a magical way of allowing you to leave something behind with every step you descend.

Imagine yourself embracing the first descend as you feel fatigue wash over you.

You may take another step down when you feel like falling deeper into a dreamy state.

Each step you take further into this deep spiral is leaving something that once distracted your mind from sleep behind on the previous step.

These distractions, thoughts, and memories that keep you awake are slowly disintegrating on the steps you already passed.

You can take another step if you want to leave another thought behind.

These thoughts don't belong in this space right here and now.

You may want to go deeper, leaving more thoughts behind for disintegration.

These thoughts won't vanish for good.

They're disappearing to a safe place where you can reach them tomorrow.

Imagine taking another step down as you feel a wave of fatigue overcome you now.

Your mind is becoming more and more blank as it can only focus on how tired you feel at this point.

Continue taking steps down this magical staircase as you descend to new depths never experienced before.

You're still in control of every step, and you can turn back any time you feel ready to come back to the verge.

It's okay if you feel enticed to go deeper and deeper.

The rest that awaits your mind is like nothing else.

The deeper you descend, the more you leave behind.

That which you leave behind will be placed in careful storage.

It won't ascend with you when you're ready to turn around.

You may want to take a few more steps down, each one allowing you to slow your mind to lower brain waves first.

You may feel your body letting go of everything that once kept you awake.

Deep sleep is calling for you now, and you want to embrace it.

Imagine yourself turning around now.

You want to come back because it's the way you find your comfortable place to sleep.

The bedroom lies at the top of the staircase again.

Allow yourself to come slowly back up the staircase, one step at a time.

The relaxation and sleepiness have completely engulfed you, and it follows you back up the stairs.

You're ready to experience every glorious moment of deep sleep as you ascend to the first curve again.

You can't let go of the deep sleep ideas, even if you want to.

One more curve will bring you to the verge again.

Take it slowly and allow your mind to ascend back into alertness, where it can only focus on sleep until tomorrow.

Feel each step as you climb, and watch the verge come nearer and nearer.

As you step onto the verge, you count to three to feel alert enough to control your mind, but you feel tired enough to fall into a deep sleep when you reach the bed.

Letting Go

This session is dedicated to anyone who needs to enhance their self-love and let go of doubt, guilt, shame, and embarrassment. It's about learning to love yourself for who you are.

Make yourself comfortable in a place of peace and quiet while you close your eyes.

You may feel an urge to escape the current space and collapse into a deeper state of mind.

My voice is here to guide you because you may have been feeling doubtful, embarrassed, or guilty about something.

It's okay to want to escape this realm that was likely painted by others.

Allow my voice to guide you gently, and feel yourself fold into a deeper state of mind with every word I speak.

Try to maintain an even breath while you listen and relax.

I want you to stretch your arms out so they are level with your eyes, and allow your palms to face towards the ground.

Just hold them here as you feel like letting yourself go deeper down this path.

Feel your body yearning for relaxation and compassion as you listen to my voice.

Imagine your arms stretching firmly as you notice how it feels like buckets are hanging from your wrists.

These buckets aren't heavy right now, and they'll only become heavier when you want them to fill more and more with water.

Listen to the dripping sounds of water flowing into the buckets, slowly and steadily.

You have permission to succumb to the sound and weight as the moments pass.

As the buckets gather more and more water, you feel yourself folding into a deeper, safer space within your mind.

You keep folding as the water levels rise, and you're welcome to start lowering your arms when you need to do so.

Lower them slowly as you fold deeper into yourself while they near the armrests.

Feel yourself succumb to a new place as your arms touch the armrests.

You're safe and protected in this space, and nothing you don't want to happen will happen.

Pause for a moment to focus on how you feel right now, and close your fist as you gently run your thumb side to side over the top of it.

You want your gentle motion to set a memory in place for the journey you're about to take.

Relax the fist again, and listen to the continuous water dripping.

Pretend you're sitting on the river bank, and there's a huge tree towering over you.

The river is as gentle as you want it to be, and the tree is whatever kind you prefer.

The dripping sound is coming from the tree above, and it misses you as the water splashes on the ground next to you.

You feel peaceful, happy, and welcome in this space.

You can feel yourself folding into a deeper comfort as you see a leaf fall from the tree.

A single leaf hits the water as you know what this leaf represents.

Pretend this leaf is the reason why you feel guilty about something, and watch as the river gently washes it downstream.

This may feel incredible as you let go of the guilt that plagued you.

Now, you see another leaf touch down on the water.

This one reminds you of a time you were embarrassed. Think about the details of why you were embarrassed.

And just like that, the leaf drifts downstream as the current carries it away from you.

You've let go of the embarrassment now, and you feel even calmer, more loved, and kinder to yourself.

Now, another leaf slowly makes its way to the water from the gigantic tree above you.

It touches down on the water, and you recognize what this leaf represents.

This leaf tells a tale of self-doubt. It shows a memory of why you feel doubtful.

And again, the current sweeps it downstream to where you can no longer see it.

Letting go of your self-doubts opens your heart and mind to a new feeling.

You feel compassionate towards yourself, and you may start thinking about how it would feel to love yourself as deeply as you deserve.

Another leaf makes it down to the water as it represents reasons why you feel ashamed of being you.

It reminds you why you think you should be ashamed of being true to yourself.

But, it quickly gets caught by the current, making its way out of sight downstream.

Pay attention to the way you feel in this moment.

You may feel a little more respect for your true self, and you may feel kindness towards the inner child brewing in your heart.

This might be the most incredible feeling you've ever experienced if you allow it to be.

Imagine yourself absorbing reasons why you matter in this world.

Imagine yourself soaking up the sun gleaming through the branches of this tree that now stands tall without the unwanted leaves.

You may feel more passionate about the true person inside of you and what this person can do.

You might feel calm in the face of knowing how much you deserve love and kindness.

You may never want those leaves to attach to your branches again.

Enjoy the experience as you allow your mind to consider new ways you should treat and respect yourself.

Let the warmth of the sun overwhelm you as you run through these ideas for what you can do to appreciate yourself more.

Feel the passion for yourself and your desires burning inside of you.

It feels impossible to leave such a compassionate place, but always remember that you're allowed to take these feelings and ideas back with you.

They belong to you. They belong to the tree above you.

Only you can decide what flows downstream when you need to let go of unwanted thoughts, beliefs, and habits again.

You may return to this tree over the river whenever you need to, but for now, you must slowly come back from this amazing place.

Welcome your new self-love back with you.

Welcome your new beliefs back into your conscious mind as you gently move away from this place.

Take five deep breaths while each one moves you closer and closer to the chair again.

The tree vanishes for now, but you're moving back into the chair that supported your journey.

Slowly open your eyes as you count quickly to five and say your waking word out loud. You might say 'awake' or 'alert.'

Pain Desensitization

This session intends to teach you how to master your pain sensors. Pain is an inevitable and unavoidable part of life, and learning how to manage it by taking control is the best way you can live with chronic or acute pain.

For a moment, I want you to close your eyes and take a nice deep breath.

Blow it out as you wait and take another deep breath.

Release this one and replace it with a third even deeper breath.

Hold this breath for a moment and move your attention to my voice.

My voice is about to guide you into a new image, and every second word allows you to fall deeper into a different state if you choose to follow it.

My voice will be gentle and kind as it takes you into a deeper state.

You're allowed to fold into yourself again and again as the words keep flowing.

You can feel your muscles sinking deeper and deeper into the chair as every second word guides you further into a calm and peaceful state.

As you continue to focus on my voice, I want you to start painting a picture in your mind now.

Paint a beautiful picture of the ocean where it meets the shore.

The waves come out to embrace the sand, and then they go back into the deeper parts of the water.

Feel yourself becoming one with the waves as you listen to my voice.

Imagine yourself flowing deeper into the ocean as though you are the ocean.

You're controlling every wave that moves in and out of the depths of this vast body of water.

You have become the body of water, flowing gently over the warm sand and going back into the depths, allowing your mind to fall deeper into itself.

Once you feel at one with the ocean, I want you to cross your fingers on your left hand and hold it for the count of five.

Allow the crossed fingers to establish how you feel as being one with the powerful body of water ebbing and flowing off the shore.

Seek a connection between this feeling and the water as you gently release your crossed fingers.

You may be feeling much calmer now. You may be feeling much deeper in the inner parts of your mind now.

But, you also feel something new.

Imagine how powerful you feel as you course on and off the shore.

The ocean is you, and the ocean is a powerful force.

You possess the power within this amazing force that brushes over the shore and back.

There's still something that bothers your waters as they feel like calmness and power combined.

There's a nagging pain when you look at the shore.

A few rocks are protruding from the sand, and they're causing discomfort in your tiding flow.

Each time your waves wash over the rocks, you feel an unwanted pain in a place only you know.

This place might often be painful, or it might be a recent discomfort from an injury.

Take a moment to focus on this space where the rocks divide the warmth of the sand.

These rocks interfere with your comfort as you flow over the sand that feels so welcoming.

There's something you need to know now.

Rocks seem like solid and unbreakable protrusions, and they can be sharp or dull.

It's nature's way of designing this landscape by placing rocks near the shores.

You feel deeply relaxed right now, and you have to realize how much control you have over this landscape.

The ocean is made of water, but there's nothing more powerful than an ocean that comprises 70 percent of the landscape.

You can do something about the rocks if you give into the power that lies within your body of water.

You can change the way these rocks disrupt your calm waves over the warm sand.

There will always be rocks, and they'll always seem like unbreakable protrusions, but the power within your waters is capable of crumbling them.

Imagine yourself as the biggest, most powerful wave of control heading straight for the rocks.

Feel the power multiply as you come closer to the shore.

Use the momentum within this giant wave to crash into the rocks, breaking them up into tiny fragments, barely able to disrupt your visits to the shore again.

Allow yourself to fall back into deeper waters as you scan the shore for more rocks.

As you spot them, you feel yourself taking charge towards the shore, gathering more and more power with every passing moment.

You may draw back into the ocean as you see these rocks crumble again.

Feel the speed and poise at which you alter the body of the ocean to your desire.

The deeper you go, the more momentum you can build for each attack on these painful rocks that form on the shore.

Knowing how well you can manage pain now, you can slowly allow yourself to follow my voice back.

Allow the image of the ocean and shore to slowly fade away as you feel the power lie within you now.

My voice gently and kindly takes you further and further away from this landscape.

There's no need to resist because the power to manage pain lies within your mind now.

You have become the ocean, so allow it to fade before it vanishes.

The entire image becomes distant enough to be unrecognizable.

You can feel yourself back in your chair, and you can pay attention to your breathing as your entire body and mind are relaxed now.

Pain might still exist, but you have power and control over it now.

Allow your eyes to open slowly as you count from five to one.

Each number brings you closer to your chair, and on the count of one, you may assertively say, "I'm alert now."

Quit Smoking or Drinking

Hypnosis is commonly used by people who would like to kick bad habits like smoking and drinking. These are not habits we want in our lives, but the subconscious mind loves sticking to old ways. This session will help you if you want to rid yourself of the unkind habits that ruin your life and health.

I would like for you to sit in a place where you won't be disturbed by noises and other distractions.

Make yourself cozy as you allow yourself to be guided gently into a deeper state if you wish.

Anchor your feet against the ground and lay your arms onto the armrests while you find something on which to focus.

Try to spot a mark on the wall where you can focus all your attention.

My voice will calmly take you deeper if you want to go deeper.

Your eyes will become tired with time as you take five deep and long breaths in and out.

Let your mind wander into a space where relaxation overtakes you while you continue watching this spot on the wall.

The spot seems so small, and it only grows more distant as your eyes grow more tired.

You may experience blinking on and off as you try to maintain your focus on this spot, which seems to be growing more and more distant now.

Is the spot growing smaller, or are your eyes growing heavier?

You may allow yourself to blink more until your eyes gently fall into a closed position.

The spot disappears behind your eyelids as you navigate your way into deeper relaxation now.

Allow my voice to keep guiding you as you fall as deep into the depths of your mind as you desire.

Every word sends you deeper, and every even breath allows your entire body to relax more and more.

Imagine yourself feeling as calm as a gentle cloud floating through the sky.

You can see all of the wonderful gardens beneath, and you can feel the warmth of the sun kissing your back as you float deeper and deeper into this space.

You may wish to keep a reminder of this space.

You may want to connect with this relaxation at any time, and you can do it now by enforcing the reminder with a simple touch.

Gently rub your index finger against your thumb, and allow this feeling or sensation to lock on to this incredible depth you've encountered.

Rub your fingers together three more times before you move your attention back to the cloud drifting through the gentle and compassionate sky.

You pass a few gardens before you reach a familiar one.

Imagine yourself floating downward to get a closer look now.

Pretend to be the cloud hanging close to this garden, waiting to see the story it tells.

There's a young child in this garden, and they look so happy and healthy.

Pay attention to the way they smile and giggle during play with their friends.

You may feel the urge to focus on the main child as you watch them run around the garden, as fit as anything.

Watch this child climb a tree, and imagine them smiling as broad as the horizon.

They look so happy. They look like nothing can change the way they feel.

This child seems to be active and sporty.

Before long, they're back on the ground, running away from their friends while playing tag.

You can't believe the speed of this child, and you recognize them more and more with each smile you see.

This child makes you think of yourself at this age.

You were such a young, wild, and active little munchkin.

Move your attention to the table next to the garage now.

On this table lies a pack of cigarettes and a bottle of alcohol.

You can feel the anger building inside of you.

Why is this within the grasp of this healthy, active young version of yourself?

Why would anyone want this beautiful child to take that bottle or light a cigarette?

Allow the anger to overwhelm you as you notice the child continues to play.

They never pay attention to the table where everything bad awaits.

They continue to run, jump, and climb, and they seem so happy with their life.

Feel the pride wash over you as you realize that this child doesn't need those terrible things.

Feel the excitement as you watch this child run away from all their friends because they're the healthiest of them all.

Allow yourself to think of an answer to a question now.

Would you allow this incredible child to touch the contents of the table, or would you rather encourage them to continue being as free as a bird?

You feel this connection to your inner child. This child represents who you were and what you could do before you adopted the habits displayed by the table.

It's okay to feel mad about the habits. It's also okay to know that it will take a little time to remove this table from the garden.

What you might feel certain about now is that you don't want this child to take those things from the table.

You want them to remain free and happy.

Indulge in the way it feels to float above this garden, knowing how you can keep your inner child safe now.

Grasp the sensations coursing through your body and mind as you feel a gentle breeze blow you back towards here and now.

You feel at peace with yourself, even if you're blowing back now.

The sounds of the children playing in the garden grow more and more distant as the wind guides you back slowly.

You may feel yourself settle back into the chair as you open your eyes.

Notice how the dot on the wall grows larger and larger with every breath you take.

Count yourself out of this state from one to five as the dot increases and doubles in size.

Everything is back to normal now, and you're completely awake.

Overcome Depression

Depression has become too common in this modern, messed up world, especially since the pandemic hit our shores. Isolation is one way people have been left to wander their thoughts too often, and most people have reasons to be depressed if given enough time to reminisce about it. What people don't need to succumb to is the overwhelming emotions that follow a depressive mood. No one deserves to be depressed, but most people succumb to this painful experience at some point in their lives. This session is specially made for anyone who needs a break from the intrusive thoughts and emotions in depression as it aims to replace them with reminders of how great it feels to be happy again.

For this session, I want you to take a walk down memory lane via a staircase.

Allow my voice to shine a light on the stairs as you walk deeper into the state you wish to reach.

Allow me to guide you gently as you descend into a better place.

Close your eyes, and imagine yourself on the verge of a staircase.

The number of stairs depends on how far you'd like to travel down to the door below.

Every step you take will slowly release negative thoughts and feelings from your mind as you descend to a deeper state.

You're permitted to fold into yourself in any way you wish as you deserve a break from this place here and now.

Take the first step down towards the door as you embrace the deepening of your mind.

Take another step as you move further away from a mind saturated with sad thoughts and memories.

You may take another step as your mind feels lighter with each one.

You're welcome to embrace the fourth step as you draw nearer to the doorway.

Feel the sensations in your body and mind as you go deeper and deeper down this staircase.

Imagine yourself putting one foot ahead of the other, and each drop in depth is deeper and deeper.

The deeper you travel down the staircase, the lighter your heart and mind feel.

You may start experiencing a sense of calmness wash over your mind as you descend once more.

Keep going if you wish because the door is as deep as you need it to be.

Once you reach the door, place your hand on the knob and gently turn it.

What appears behind the door is entirely up to you.

There's only one rule about what comes next.

I want you to imagine yourself reentering a fond memory.

I want you to choose the memory you hold dearest.

When ready, you can walk through the doorway and into this memory that once made you feel butterflies in your stomach.

Perhaps you revisited your favorite vacation spot.

Maybe you entered the doorway to a childhood memory where your grandma was baking cookies in the kitchen.

Perhaps you're revisiting a time you accomplished something you never dreamed of completing.

Whatever lies beyond the door is within your control now.

Take a brief moment to install a shortcut to this memory.

You may touch your left arm with your right hand, or you may pull your ear gently for three seconds before you continue to this amazing place.

Now, let go of the shortcut and enter the memory completely.

Replay the memory that you chose for this place.

Allow it to play out as it did when you were first here.

Recognize the faces you saw in your first experience, whether it's grandma's smile or your friend's grin as you sat on the warm beach sand.

Smell the cookies if you're revisiting grandma, or listen to the applause fill the room if you're revisiting the memory of accomplishment.

Take note of every detail in the memory, and allow all your senses to fold deep into your mind as you watch the memory play again and again.

You can hear all the sounds you once loved, and you can see all the people who share this memory with you.

You may even taste the cookies, or reminisce about the tender embrace from your partner on vacation.

Feel the safety, warmth, happiness, and utter excitement of this journey.

You may experience every happy emotion all over again.

You're allowed to embrace the excitement of the day, and you may soak up all the joy of laughing with your friends.

This is now your safe place.

Whatever you designed behind the door is what you can return to any time you feel sad again.

What you created in this place will uplift your mood every time you think about it.

You'll feel cherished, loved, and absolute joy when you touch your arm again.

Everyone in this memory plays a role in your emotions.

Allow them to be part of your journey to feeling better each day.

Allow all the sensory information to follow you back into the staircase.

When you're done experiencing the joy of this memory, again and again, you may come back to the door.

You'll always be able to revisit this place, so come back now.

Feel the knob turn in your hand again before walking through the door.

Gently shut the door behind you as your new emotions and thoughts become a part of you.

Take the first step up towards the verge on which you stood, and follow it with another step.

Continue ascending the stairs, knowing that you have what you need to embrace the challenges at the top without succumbing to the bad notions again.

Take another step as you feel the smile reaching from ear to ear across your face.

Walk tall with your chest out as you carry the new mood with you.

As you near the top of the staircase, take a moment to pause and allow the positive and happy sensations to overwhelm you.

Feel your foot connect to the final step as you assert your waking state again.

Push yourself over the verge as you count back from three, and say, "I'm awake and alert now."

Overcome Anxiety

Anxiety is just another shared problem in this new world, and it helps if we have ways to manage our fears and uncertainties. Fear is a hellishly strong emotion, and it can hold you back from reaching out to better opportunities. This session will help you see your fears from a new perspective so you can overcome them. Remember that hypnosis allows you to desensitize yourself to fears and other problems, so you can be assured that listening to a session like this one often will slowly expose you to things you normally avoid out of anxiousness.

I want you to start this session differently. Gently shake your arms before sitting down and closing your eyes. This gets the blood flowing before you go to a deeper place.

Now, you may listen to my voice if you choose to go deeper.

Close your eyes gently and without force, as you draw a deep and even breath into your lungs.

Expel this breath slowly as you focus on the way it feels as it exits your lungs.

Now, take another deep breath as you feel a deeper sense of relaxation enter your body through your nose, and hold this breath for two seconds.

Expel the air as it pushes out any ideas of resistance if you desire to deepen your state.

Take another breath in through the nose and hold it while you realize this is the third breath cycle.

Expelling it allows your mind and body to sink deeper and deeper into the chair beneath you.

Take the fourth breath into your nose, and try to draw this one even deeper into your core now.

Hold it for two seconds before you expel it as you sink deeper into your chair.

My voice is becoming calmer and allowing you to descend deeper if you wish.

Now, take the fifth breath deep into your nose and down into your belly. Try to hold this one for three seconds while you feel the calmness circling your mind.

I want you to expel this long and deep breath faster than the others as you feel overwhelmed by the comfort beneath you.

You may welcome the comfort as your mind has descended into a depth you previously thought impossible.

Just allow this depth and the comfort that comes with it to engulf you for a moment.

Realize how powerful the depth is in taking away your worries, and embed this state within your mind now.

Create a circle with your index finger and thumb, and hold the circle for the count of five before releasing it.

This allows you to embed a bookmark for the upcoming changes.

Now, allow my voice to make suggestions, and allow your mind to customize the suggestions to what you need to face in your life.

Everyone has a secret fear hidden in the depths of their minds.

Imagine yourself standing in front of a large cage.

The cage is reinforced with the strongest metals in the world, and slowly, you can see something taking shape inside the cage.

There's no need to fear what manifests in this space because you feel a little more courageous with each passing moment.

You feel bravery touching your innermost parts as the form takes shape.

Slowly, the prisoner of this cage starts resembling that which you fear.

Bravely, you watch as it transforms into what makes you anxious.

You can feel your courage doubling every moment as the fear grows inside the cage.

It can't reach you in this safe space.

This space was designed for you to see your fear manifest.

It doesn't matter if you fear failure at work.

It doesn't matter if your anxiety surrounds meeting someone new.

Perhaps your fear is a tangible object that you can't avoid.

Maybe you fear driving, or perhaps you fear the spiders crawling about your apartment in the night.

Whatever your fear is within your mind, it's slowly taking a physical shape in the cage.

It cannot reach you, and you cannot feel the normal anxiety this thing causes you.

You may even take a step closer to examine it from the safety behind the cage.

Embrace the courage to move closer to it.

Embrace the bravery installing itself in the deepest part of your mind.

Nothing can make you fear it in this place in which you feel a new sense of security.

You might want to allow a single fear to manifest this time. You can always revisit this place by recreating your circle to deepen yourself again.

Take another step forward if you wish, and stare your uncertainty in the face.

Don't force yourself if you feel hesitant.

One day, you may be able to revisit this same cage that holds your fears, and you might even be able to open it, stepping inside the cage with what used to make you scared.

For now, you can simply watch it, study it, and realize how it has less and less power over you.

Absorb every ounce of courage you can collect in this magical place before you step away from the cage.

Feel the courage coursing through your veins, allowing you to switch off any response in the brain as you wish.

Imagine yourself moving away from the cage slowly now.

Move your focus back to the way your breath moves calmly and evenly through you to bring yourself back.

All the courage you gained thus far is traveling back with you.

It belongs to you, and the fear will slowly lessen over time.

Notice yourself take the fifth breath as you're about to count your way out of this place.

The fourth breath makes the cage seem smaller and more distant.

The third breath brings you back to your chair where everything is better now.

The second breath allows your body and mind to latch onto the weight of where you are again.

And the final breath brings you back while you open your eyes and remind yourself that you're alert and awake now.

Managing Grief

Grief is a broad word that includes losing loved ones, jobs, and a previous lifestyle. Loss is a better word if you want to include the wide range of people and things we can lose. Losing loved ones is a painful change in your life, and some people can struggle with the loss of a job, security, and even something as simple as an old habit. This session is dedicated to anyone suffering a loss they can't manage. This session will also use a candle flame for eye fixation, but please ensure the candle is secure so it won't fall over. Place the candle in a wide base holder, and use a thick candle that can't tip over. Make sure it's also placed on a table away from curtains. You're most welcome to use a scented candle as it will double your sensory experience. The reason why we use a candle for grief induction is that it's also a ritual we tend to practice when we light candles for lost loved ones.

This is a very deep session that brings us close to something we crave about a loss or change we endured.

I want you to sit back and take three gentle breaths to clear your mind.

Allow the air to pass through you, calming every fiber of your being as it passes.

Now, pay attention to the candle flame as you go deeper into this experience, only so much as you desire.

I want you to pause thoughts about your loss briefly as you allow my calm and compassionate voice to take you slightly deeper with every breath you take.

Every muscle in your body will loosen as you fall deeper and deeper.

Maintain your focus on the candle flame, and watch as it dances back and forth.

Try to find a rhythm in the flame, which will also dance you into a deeper state.

Imagine the doubled effect of the dancing flame combined with my voice, taking you deeper and deeper into a calm state where everything will look different.

Take another breath, and draw it down into the depths of your core as you continue watching the flame and listening to my voice.

Draw another deeper breath that touches your core as you start realizing how your eyes are growing heavier.

You may start blinking now, and that's okay.

This is a peaceful place you're about to enter, and you may go as deep into it as you desire.

Take one more breath before your eyes grow heavy enough to fall closed.

You may still be able to see the flame dancing behind your tired eyes now.

Allow my voice to take you to an even deeper place as you feel your entire body collapse into the surface beneath you.

Notice how every muscle lets go of the flame slowly as you fall deeper and deeper.

Pretend as though you still have some muscle control in your fingers so you can leave a shortcut in this most relaxing space.

All you need is a little muscle control to touch your little finger against your thumb.

Hold this finger-touch position for a moment as you feel yourself falling into a deeper, more peaceful place where they gently move apart from each other over the next three seconds.

Now, you may feel as deep as you want to reach, and you may follow my voice as I guide you to a new place.

Imagine yourself sitting in a car riding gently down the interstate.

You may be the driver, or you may allow me to drive.

This interstate is familiar. It's the same interstate your life takes every morning to reach the destination on the other end every evening.

You may look at the exits as you pass them, and you'll recognize many of them.

You pass the morning exit where you have breakfast.

You may pass an exit where you visit the gym.

You don't need to take these exits right now.

You may continue driving until you see pop-up exits along your route.

These pop-up exits are called "memory banks."

As soon as you feel ready, take the first memory exit to visit the place that no longer is tangible in your life beyond the mental interstate.

Allow yourself to follow the exit until you reach a familiar place.

It may be a place you visited with a loved one you lost. It may be a place where you once worked.

This place is frozen in time, and you may visit it again and again if you take the memory exits.

Drive as close to the memory as you can, and engage with it.

Take a moment to watch your loved one smiling. You may even get out of the car if you want to physically engage with them.

Embrace them, and pay attention to the sensations coursing through you as you touch them.

Your memories are safe in this place, and you may listen to their laughter. You may engage with them in every way inside this space.

These memory exits only have one rule.

You may not stay longer than 10 minutes, or you won't reach the destination at the end of the interstate.

Your loved one may even remind you it's time to go, and they'll reassure you how peaceful it is in this memory bank.

This may feel uncomfortable, but you must let them go.

You can revisit these memory exits as often as you need to, but you need to get back on the interstate now.

Imagine giving your loved one the longest hug before getting back in the car.

Imagine seeing them smile broadly as you leave them frozen in this beautiful place.

Memory exits often take you to the most beautiful memories you have to share with this person.

As hard as it may seem, you need to start your engine and put the car into drive.

You may visit them tomorrow, and perhaps you visit them in a different memory exit next time, but you have to get back on the interstate.

It's okay to feel emotional as you drive away.

This allows the person to see the human side of you.

You're allowed to be sad, but watch your loved one's peaceful face in the rear-view mirror as you turn back onto the interstate.

You may even feel a tear run down your face, but the interstate is a magical place.

Soon enough, you're passing exits to regular daily routines again.

You may even notice new exits, which means new opportunities are starting to appear on your route.

Allow your mood to slowly improve while you drive down your interstate, watching all the new exits popping up.

Some exits are more memories, but you should only visit one a day.

Other exits may even remind you of all that for which you have to be grateful.

Some exits may remind you to smile when you consider how well your life has progressed since the loss.

This journey down your interstate is merely a passing state.

You're nearing the end of the interstate now, and you may see the flame dancing back and forth again.

The flame lights your way to the end of the interstate now, and my voice will gently guide you back into the chair.

Breathe deeply and evenly as you near the flame, allowing yourself to slowly count back from five to one.

On the count of one, the flame becomes static again, allowing your eyes to spring open, and you're fully alert in your chair.

Anger Management

Anger is another emotion we often face, and this session will allow you to face your anger before expelling it the wrong way. This session will allow you to expel it in the only acceptable place.

I want you to sit as relaxed as you can and close your eyes.

Hear my voice as I guide you down a path that takes you deeper and deeper into a new place.

Allow your body to rise and fall as you calmly and evenly breathe in and out.

Raise your arms to stretch in front of you, and allow your palms to face the floor.

I want you to hold your arms out like this as you continue breathing and paying attention to my voice.

Feel yourself letting go for a moment as every weight you carry slowly moves down into your arms.

The less weight your body contains, the deeper you fold into your mind.

The more weight your arms gain, the deeper you fall into this new space.

Your breathing may start slowing down as your heart finds a new rhythm.

You feel an urge to allow your arms to settle, but you want to keep them as high as possible for as long as you can.

Your heart's rhythm steadily grows slower and more even as your arms become heavier and heavier.

You may start allowing your arms to slowly succumb under the weight.

Every inch your arms move down to your sides allows your mind to double its depth into this new realm.

Draw a deep breath before your arms reach the midpoint of their descent.

Notice how relaxed your body feels as your arms lower deeper and deeper.

As your arms touch the armrests, you can feel your mind fall into itself.

Allow your head to fall back into the chair as your mind is deeper than before.

Allow my voice to show you how calm and relaxed you may be feeling now.

Calmness rushes over your mind as you sink into the chair beneath you.

This is an incredible feeling where anger doesn't exist.

It's a calm place where your mind can wander down a relaxing path.

I want you to cross the big toe over your second toe on either foot now.

Feel the connection between the toes and how peaceful the big toe rests on the smaller toe.

This feeling will remind you of this calm space you're in right now when you need it again. Count to three and release the toes now.

Imagine you're standing inside of a boxing ring.

At this point, you still feel calm and collected, but that only lasts until an opponent steps into your ring.

This opponent is anyone or anything that gets your rage amped up again.

It's okay to experience the rage for a moment while you realize you have boxing gloves on your hands.

Whatever you do to this person in this mental ring will not hurt them in another place.

This is the only place you may expel your anger on this person or thing that upsets you.

Pretend as though you feel the power coursing through your arms now.

Do you want to punch this person or thing?

Do you want to lash out to expel the rage from your heart and mind?

Allow yourself to do what you want, and feel the rage transfer to the object as you lay your gloves deep into the thing that makes you so mad.

Notice how it feels when you step back.

You may feel calmer, or you may feel the need to lay it on this object again.

Step forth, and deliver another punch as mighty as you can.

Focus on the rage flowing out of your gloves and into the object that once made you so angry.

Step back again as you pay attention to the way your rage feels less and less.

It's okay if you want to step forth once more to deliver the final blow.

You're in control here, and you may release the final rage within your gloves.

Step back again, and imagine yourself feeling complete freedom from the anger you once held.

Pretend as though you're feeling on top of the world, and best of all is you never had to deliver a real punch in the outside world.

Imagine yourself falling backward into a comfortable and safe space where all the rage is gone now.

The object or person who made you angry might still be in the ring if you want, but they don't make you angry anymore.

The sight of this person or thing brings no rage into your gloves, which have now vanished.

You feel calm, peaceful, and happy.

Take a few moments to cherish the incredible serenity the freedom from rage creates.

Imagine the peaceful feelings washing over you now.

Whatever anger you held is gone, and you can't be angry at this person or object anymore.

Even if you try, you won't feel angry at them again.

Take this amazing feeling back with you as you start your backward journey.

The ring vanishes, and you find yourself sitting back in the chair.

Feel the comfort engulfing you as you count back from 10 to one slowly.

Each count brings more and more weight back into your body.

The weight slowly moves away from your arms and back into your core.

Keep counting as you reach five.

You can even raise your hands now without the weight that held them down.

You may reach the count of three now as you slowly open your eyes.

By the count of one, you pull your head forward from the headrest and feel fully and completely awake.

Confidence Void of Jealousy

One of the main reasons why we feel like we're not good enough or we can't do what others do is that our self-beliefs are guided by jealousy. Jealousy was never innate in our childhood. It's something we learned from those around us. It's an environmental hypnosis factor that only multiplies in this world of social media and Instagram influencers. However, allowing jealousy to guide our ships is a mistake. We can't be confident if we're always envious of someone else's life. This session will help you gather confidence and forget about the jealousy the environment loves imprinting in your mind.

I want you to close your eyes as you sink into the chair holding your absolute comfort.

You may focus on my voice as you're about to enter a deeper state, where a new experience excitedly awaits you.

You may take calm and even breaths as you continue to sink a little deeper into the chair with each one.

I want you to use your incredible imagination to pretend as though you're standing at the top of a staircase, leading down to a place where the magic happens.

Slowly, put your foot onto the second step as you desire a deeper and closer look at this place.

Notice how you sink deeper and deeper into a peaceful state as you descend another step and another one.

Continue making your way down the steps as the depth is entirely in your hands.

Allow yourself to be drawn to the magic happening in this deeper level below.

Follow the attraction you may be feeling to the bottom of the staircase as you continue to take even paces down the steps.

Each step allows your mind to wander deeper into the state it may achieve.

Follow the steps further and further down until you reach the depth you're comfortable with, and then you can see what lies at the bottom.

You reach the final step down, and you take five deep breaths before your eyes meet the place you're supposed to reach.

You've walked down into a stage where everyone can be who they wish to be, but everyone should be them true selves.

This deep level that meets the stage makes you feel relaxed, calm, and of a new mind.

I want you to gently bite your lower lip. Don't bite it so hard it hurts.

Allow your upper teeth to rest gently on your bottom lip, and hold this position for three seconds to remind you about the experience you're about to step into.

Once the moments pass, pay attention to the clothes you're wearing.

You look fabulous in every way, and you even have your favorite colors on to boost your confidence.

Imagine yourself slowly understanding what this stage is.

The people in the crowd are those with whom you feel most comfortable.

These people make you feel at ease.

There are two people ahead of you in this contest of authenticity.

Each person must walk onto the stage and recite something amazing about themselves.

The winner will be the most authentic person.

Watch the two people ahead of you as they express their greatest talents.

Pretend as though you're becoming more and more excited to see the flaws in their stories.

These were perhaps people you once envied for their better lives.

You may have once felt a deep sense of jealousy when you first watched them.

However, this crowd is a magical one, capable of seeing the truth behind their stories.

The crowd's applause volume is what determines the winner of this contest.

Now, it's your turn.

Step onto the stage in your most glorious and confident outfit as you may feel slight resistance.

It's okay to feel nervous. It doesn't mean you lack confidence.

It's time to tell your story.

Imagine yourself starting to say what makes you unique and valuable as you pay close attention to the faces in the crowd.

Your confidence grows as you see the faces light up with intrigue, curiosity, and amazement.

Keep telling your story as the crowd moves forward on their seats.

Notice how your confidence doubles and even trebles with every passing moment.

You have the crowd in your hands now, and they love your story.

They love how authentic and unique you are in every way.

Imagine the crowd giving you a standing ovation at the end of your story.

Pretend as though the stage vibrates with the roar of the crowd.

There's a clear winner of this contest, and it's well-deserved.

Take a moment to recognize how you feel right now.

Pay attention to how your mind and heart feel free from the jealousy that once disturbed you.

You may feel more confident in yourself than you've ever been before.

There will never be a need to compare yourself to others again, even once you make your way back up the staircase.

Spend a few moments in this glory before you slowly turn back to the staircase.

You may find your foot reaching the first step as you feel the stage growing a little distant now.

The stage grows more and more distant with every step you take towards the top of the staircase.

The feelings you gained on the stage follow you up the staircase, and you feel yourself coming back slowly as you keep ascending the stairs.

Feel yourself rising in confidence and awakening at the same time as you pass the halfway mark up the stairs.

Return your focus to your breathing as you near the end of the staircase.

Imagine your foot grounding itself solidly on the last step as you count to five.

On the count of five, you feel yourself reawakening completely.

Stress Freedom

Stress has to be the most common contender we face. It's not just things we fear or things that pose a danger that makes us activate the sympathetic nervous system. It's also the stress that pushes us to finish things on time and prepare for potential hurdles on our paths. Whatever stress you face, it can be managed better with hypnosis. This session will do just that. You'll also be introduced to another form of rapid induction called the elevator.

Fall into the wrapped comfort of your chair as you're about to take another journey to a place free from stress and daily worries.

This will be a long and deep journey, but you'll decide how deep you're willing to sink into this place.

Close your eyes as you allow my voice to speak directly to your deepest mind.

You may relax your body, and take a few breaths into the bottom of your core before slowly pushing it back out.

Take another slow and steady breath that flows all the way down to your deepest parts and back up through your mouth.

Allow yourself to give way to another deep breath that travels deeper and deeper.

Feel your mind folding into itself like a box folding over and over to fall deeper and deeper into yourself.

You might feel your body releasing all the weight and tension it once held as you continue allowing your mind to fold into itself.

Every breath you take will only make it fold more and more, taking you deeper and deeper.

I want you to imagine yourself in an elevator now.

Imagine yourself standing in front of the buttons of an elevator.

When you're ready to fall even deeper into your mind, you may press the button to close the door.

Pretend as though you're on the top floor of the tallest building you can imagine, and allow the elevator to move down to the deeper parts of your mental tower.

Press the button to move five floors down as you allow the feeling of a falling elevator to succumb your mind into a newer depth.

You may feel your mind and body falling without gravity to reach a lower state.

You have no reason to be afraid of deeper levels because this is your mental tower.

Every floor is made of what you desire.

Every floor contains fragments of memory, thoughts, emotions, beliefs, and habits.

This tower is you, and you are the tower.

Allow the elevator to drop into lower levels as you feel yourself become lighter and lighter.

Feel the incredible sensations of this moving giant that allows your top mind to reach the bottom mind.

Each level you drop will only treble your depth and allow your mind to fold into itself more and more.

Now, the elevator can stop at the floor you chose because you're always in control of how deep you sink into your mind.

Imagine looking at the floor number on the panel, and feeling the incredible sensations in this deeper state.

You can feel calmer. You may feel the deepest parts of your mind relax everything about you.

Now, I want you to take your right index finger and bury it between your left index finger and thumb.

This simple little anchor will allow you to revisit this deeper, calmer place as you wish.

It will remind you of everything to come.

It will give you the key to remember how only you control this elevator.

Hold this position of your fingers until you feel the anchor set deep into your mind, and then you can release it.

Take a step closer to the panel of buttons while you take another deep and long breath into your core.

You may begin to feel the control you have over this elevator now.

You may know how much you can control in the depths of your mind now.

However, you're still many floors above the ground.

Between yourself and the lowest levels of your mind lies many habits, beliefs, and especially, things that make your deepest mind worry enough to switch your fight or flight response on.

These are the floors you want to visit.

You may start your journey now by choosing a floor that contains something you find challenging.

What task makes you feel inadequate or nervous?

Choose the floor number and imagine yourself gaining more and more confidence to face this challenge as the elevator descends into the deeper parts of your mind.

Feel yourself let go of the nervousness as the elevator reaches the desired floor.

Opening the door is up to you now.

You may press the button to open the door as soon as you're ready.

What lies beyond the door is the task that makes you feel threatened.

Imagine seeing whatever threatens your perfectly calm state of mind in the corridor of the floor you chose.

Perhaps you're afraid of messing a huge account up at work.

Maybe you feel nervous about the new challenge you're about to embrace with your relationship.

Imagine any challenge beyond this door, and examine it as you realize how the challenge seems less and less frightening.

You could first understand how the deepest mind wanted to flee from this challenge, but there's a new calmness flowing through your mind now.

The calmness grows with every second you stare at this challenge.

Once the power this challenge holds over you is reduced to nothing, you may press the button to close the door again.

Now, I want you to choose another floor, one which also holds dangerous power over your deeper mind.

Press the button when you're ready, and allow yourself to meet with this floor as the elevator sends you deeper and deeper.

You may take another deep breath as the elevator comes to a standstill.

Now, it's your decision whether you want to open the door or not.

If you want to see what this stressful floor holds, punch the door opening button now.

Another situation lies beyond the door as it opens slowly.

This one might be about the stress surrounding the new business idea you have.

Maybe the idea of starting a business is a huge feat for you.

That's okay; you may examine this stressful trigger and watch as it grows smaller and smaller.

The sensations you feel on this level are different from the last floor.

You feel a sense of acceptance in this space, knowing that a new business will be stressful.

You may also accept an additional understanding that this stress can be managed.

Imagine how many stressful situations the most successful people had to endure.

Take another breath as the door starts closing slowly while you recognize how much you need to manage the stress on this floor.

You find yourself standing in the elevator, wondering which floor comes next.

The last floor only made you realize how some stressors can't be avoided, but they can be managed.

You may need to go up a few floors this time, but there is a special floor with some answers.

Press the button to ascend to a slightly higher floor without disturbing your deep state of mind.

The deepest mind remains awake right now, but you may want to see what you can do to make the stress and challenges on other floors manageable.

The elevator slowly moves up the floors, and you may feel a sense of calmness overwhelm you again as you realize that the answers are within this building.

The elevator comes to a stop as you breathe in and out to remind yourself of how relaxed you still feel.

Everything in this building is under your control, and you may press the button to open the door when you feel ready.

Breathe in and out evenly as the door opens to a room filled with ideas.

You may see yourself sitting at a desk in the corner, planning your steps forward to ensure fewer issues with your new business.

You may also see yourself in the back-left corner of the room, writing on a blackboard.

The triggers for the most common reasons why you stress are noted on this blackboard.

You may also see another version of yourself in the center of the room, which looks like a small gym.

This part of you is controlling their stress with exercise.

Another version of you stands to the left of the room, and they look like they're practicing a gentle and relaxing hypnosis session.

Another version of you may stand to the right of the room, and this person seems to be delegating chores or responsibilities to some other people.

This entire floor is but one level that connects you to various ways to manage stress.

It's a place where answers are seen in plain sight, and you're welcome to revisit it after visiting any floor of your tower.

Take a breath into your lungs as you draw a smile on your face, and press the air out of your mouth gently as the doors close.

This tower is yours, and you may come back whenever you need to calm down.

The deepest mind is allowed to travel to higher floors so that it consumes the information there.

Now, it's time to come back to the penthouse where your conscious mind takes control again.

Press the button to elevate yourself to the highest floor as you feel your mind slowly waking with each ascending level.

You may have three floors remaining as you feel your body and mind come nearer and nearer to each other.

On the top floor, you feel yourself detach from the elevator now.

You're back in your chair, and you're slowly opening your eyes.

I'm going to count to three, and on the number three, you'll wake up completely.

Count with me. One, two, and three, and you're wide awake.

Conclusion

What you once thought was a fallacy has now become a reality. The days where you feel out of control are gone. The days you think you can't manage the direction of your life are gone. The days you feel like a failure, even if it holds no truth in other people's eyes, are now gone, too. It's amazing how we reach places in our lives where we feel confused. Who truly knows the direction of their lives, and who can control it? People who practice hypnosis are more capable of directing their lives than most. Not knowing what to do, think, or feel is as common as the grains of sand on a beach. Everyone has dreams and ambitions, but very few people are able to achieve what they desire. They struggle to take the steps they need to grow their potential.

Figure 10

Sometimes, what stands in their way is a mental block, comprising depression, stress, anxiety, and self-doubt. The worst always comes when people can't recognize who installed these beliefs. They have no idea how they came to think of themselves the way they do. All they know is that their lives are a persistent pattern of the same behaviors that bring them no closer to their dreams. Sometimes, the habits are easy to recognize. They can't be an Olympic athlete if they smoke, but how do they quit a habit they've enjoyed for years? They can't be an executive in the corporate world because they think no one pays attention to their opinions. They even doubt themselves when opportunities arise for entrepreneurial ventures.

Habits are any recurring thought, behavior, feeling, or decision we tend to repeat, even if we don't see how damaging they can be. We know that these habits don't bring us closer to our goals, but we continue to repeat them anyway. It's a sad cycle that never ends unless you awaken the minds to function together. It's a tragic tale unless you take back control over the driving forces of your behaviors. Everyone gets knocked down from time to time. Maybe you experienced a loss that left you unable to find direction after it happened. Perhaps you were diagnosed with a condition you can't change. Maybe you made a decision that didn't go as planned. Whatever happens, every person will stumble.

It's the people who control their minds, behaviors, habits, beliefs, and thoughts that stand up, again and again. They don't allow defeat to exist in their life journey, and they'll always dust themselves off again. Even the strongest beast will stumble, but whether he gets up is entirely up to the way he masters control over his mind. Human minds are powerful beyond understanding, but they still belong to us. They still make up part of our design, so we can be the powerful force that drives what goes in and out of the mind. We can be the connection between the different minds to pull them back together so that external forces can no longer pull them apart. We can be the mediator that eases tensions when new habits are introduced. The best way we can do this is by practicing self-hypnosis.

Self-hypnosis allows us to be the mediator, connection, and master of everything that happens. You've learned about the minds now, and you understand how they function in their own rights. You also know how the environment has conditioned you over your life span, and you recognize the way it can be stopped. Every belief within your mind can be questioned now. Does it belong to the true inner child inside of you, or has it been installed by societal factory settings? You don't need anymore evidence to see how hypnosis has worked in science, and you have everything necessary to establish your new routine, which includes daily self-hypnosis sessions. You know how to use the right suggestions that work for you, and you can induce yourself without paying thousands for hypnotherapy.

You also know what neuro-linguistic programming and the laws of attraction can do for you. You may find new answers with your role-play exercise, and you might learn to invest in the right things now. You know how to choose your goals, and you know how to assure that they belong to you, so you can invest them where they matter now. You know how to look after your physical, mental, and emotional health now with small lifestyle changes, and you can use your dreams as a gateway to and from your subconscious mind. The sessions cover the most common problems, and you can always use them to inspire your own recordings. You'll always have full control over your depth, session-type, and suggestions.

There's no need to allow this world and all its challenges to derail you from becoming your best self anymore. You have everything you need to design hypnosis sessions that work personally for you. You can also design sessions to promote your work life and career. I'd love to hear from you once you finished this book. Feel free to leave a comment or review to let me know if my guidance helped you. I wish to write more books about this incredible practice, and your comments could help me understand what else people need to know. You can even simply leave a 'hello' to let me and others know whether this book helped you in the ways you needed.

My final piece of caring advice to you is that you open your mind to new possibilities every day. Don't remain stuck in the same place you were yesterday. Aim to improve yourself and your life each day, even if it's with one tiny change. Now, go out there and create a storm of changes!

References

Assaraf, J. (n.d.). *Innercise: How to find the motivation to accomplish anything.* My NeuroGym. https://blog.myneurogym.com/video-innercise-motivation/

Brooks, S. (2019, April 4). *31 hypnosis techniques (the most comprehensive list).* British Hypnosis Research. https://britishhypnosisresearch.com/hypnosis-techniques/

Cherry, K. (2020, June 26). *Erik Erikson's stages of psychosocial development.* Verywell Mind. https://www.verywellmind.com/erik-eriksons-stages-of-psychosocial-development-2795740

Cherry, K., & Gans, S. (2019). *What impact did Gestalt psychology have?* Verywell Mind. https://www.verywellmind.com/what-is-gestalt-psychology-2795808

Cherry, K., & Gans, S. (2020, December 9). *The structure and levels of the mind according to Freud.* Verywell Mind. https://www.verywellmind.com/the-conscious-and-unconscious-mind-2795946#:~:text=The%20Preconscious%2C%20Conscious%2C%20and%20Unconscious%20Minds

Chris, M. (2014, November 24). *How to use anchors in hypnosis and NLP for building confidence.* Brain Director. https://www.braindirector.com/how-to-use-anchors-in-hypnosis-and-nlp-for-building-confidence/

Cohen, J. (2019, April 22). Hypnosis: Is it worth the hype? *Forbes.* https://www.forbes.com/sites/jennifercohen/2019/04/22/hypnosis-is-it-worth-the-hype/?sh=70c50daf3ca8

Costa, A. L., & Kallick, B. (2019). *Brain development in children 2 to 7.* ASCD. http://www.ascd.org/publications/books/119017/chapters/Brain-Development-in-Children-2-to-7.aspx

Ducey, J. (2018). *How to use your journal to hypnotize yourself & reprogram your subconscious | the law of attraction* [Video]. YouTube. https://www.youtube.com/watch?v=v0Ay3L9K5j8

Fogan, S. (2016, March 31). Welcome: Hypnotherapy, low-blood sugar levels and agoraphobia. *Welcome.* http://calminsensehypnotherapy.blogspot.com/2016/03/hypnotherapy-low-blood-sugar-levels-and.html

Folen's Publishers. (2009). *Chapter 3 the psychodynamic approach.* The Women's Center. https://www.thewomenscentre.co.uk/wp-content/uploads/2015/11/WJEC_AS_Ch_03.pdf

Ford, A. (2015, March 10). "Tranceformation:" David Spiegel on how hypnosis can change your brain's perception of your body. *Scope.* https://scopeblog.stanford.edu/2015/03/10/tranceformation-david-spiegel-on-how-hypnosis-can-change-your-brains-perception-of-your-body/

Fulcher, R. Z. (2018, December 14). Developing your "hypnotic voice" - how to talk like a hypnotherapist. *HypnoTC.* https://hypnotc.com/hypnotic-voice/

Good Therapy. (2016, February 2). *Dream analysis.* Good Therapy. https://www.goodtherapy.org/learn-about-therapy/types/dream-analysis#:~:text=During%20dream%20analysis%2C%20the%20person

Gordon, D. (2002). *David Gordon.* Ericksonian Info. https://ericksonian.info/author/david/#:~:text=About%20David%20Gordon

Halsband, U., Mueller, S., Hinterberger, T., & Strickner, S. (2009). Plasticity changes in the brain in hypnosis and meditation. *Contemporary Hypnosis,* *26*(4), 194–215. https://doi.org/10.1002/ch.386

Harvard Health Publishing. (2018, May 1). *Understanding the stress response.* Harvard Health. https://www.health.harvard.edu/staying-healthy/understanding-the-stress-response

Harvard Medical School. (2019). *Consequences of insufficient sleep | healthy sleep.* Harvard. http://healthysleep.med.harvard.edu/healthy/matters/consequences

Hellebrand, S. (n.d.). *About hypnotherapy.* Hypnosis Motivation. https://www.hypnosismotivation.com/about-hypnotherapy/

Henley, J. (2020, December 21). *Deepening techniques to deepen the trance experience - deep trance.* Dr. James Henley. https://www.drjameshenley.us/deep-trance/deepening-techniques.html

History of Hypnosis. (2019a). *James Braid | history of hypnosis.* History of Hypnosis. http://www.historyofhypnosis.org/james-braid.html

History of Hypnosis. (2019b). *Milton H. Erickson | history of hypnosis.* History of Hypnosis. http://www.historyofhypnosis.org/milton-erickson.html

Hypnosis Motivation Institute. (2021a). *The birth of mesmerism - hypnosis in history.* Hypnosis Motivation Institute. https://hypnosis.edu/history/the-birth-of-mesmerism

Hypnosis Motivation Institute. (2021b). *The mental bank ledger - John G. Kappas, Ph.D. - HMI bookstore.* Hypnosis Motivation Institute. https://hypnosis.edu/books/mental-bank-ledger

Hypnotherapy Center. (2019, August 9). *432 Hz the frequency of the universe.* Hypnosis and Hypnotherapy Center. https://hypnotherapycenter.co.za/432-hz-the-frequency-of-the-universe/

International Hypnosis Association. (n.d.). *Code of ethics and conduct.* International Hypnosis Association. https://www.hypnosiscredentials.com/code-of-ethics/

Interpersonal Hypnotherapy. (2018, July 24). *US state hypnosis laws.* Interpersonal Hypnotherapy. https://www.interpersonalhypnotherapy.com/us-state-hypnosis-laws#:~:text=

Khoshaba, D. (2012, March 27). *A seven-step prescription for self-love.* Psychology Today. https://www.psychologytoday.com/za/blog/get-hardy/201203/seven-step-prescription-self-love

Kröner-Borowik, T., Gosch, S., Hansen, K., Borowik, B., Schredl, M., & Steil, R. (2013). The effects of suppressing intrusive thoughts on dream content, dream distress and psychological parameters. *Journal of Sleep Research, 22*(5), 600–604. https://doi.org/10.1111/jsr.12058

Krouwel, M. (2020, June 5). Hypnotic deepeners - what are they and when might you use them. *Matthew Krouwel Hypnotherapist.* https://matt-hypnotherapist.co.uk/hypnotic-deepeners/

Lally, P., van Jaarsveld, C. H. M., Potts, H. W. W., & Wardle, J. (2009). How are habits formed: Modelling habit formation in the real world. *European Journal of Social Psychology, 40*(6), 998–1009. https://doi.org/10.1002/ejsp.674

Lauren. (2020, August 14). Mental bank | free ledger & more | your financial freedom journey. *Lauren's Financial Freedom.* https://www.laurensfinancialfreedomjourney.com/mental-bank/

Laves-Webb, L. (2020, February 3). Dream therapy: Types of dreams and how to interpret them. *Louis Laves-Webb*. https://www.louislaves-webb.com/dream-therapy/

Ledochowski, I. (2016, March 29). 15 highly effective hypnotic power words to influence others. *Hypnosis Training Academy*. https://hypnosistrainingacademy.com/3-surefire-power-words-to-gain-power-and-influence-people-fast/

Marchant, J. (2013). Those resistant to "love hormone" may also be easier to hypnotize. *Nature*. https://doi.org/10.1038/nature.2013.12836

Margolies, L. (2016, May 17). *Making decisions: Evolved or primitive brain?* Psych Central. https://psychcentral.com/lib/how-to-tell-if-your-decisions-are-from-your-evolved-or-primitive-brain-2#4

Mcleod, S. (2019). *Unconscious mind.* Simply Psychology. https://www.simplypsychology.org/unconscious-mind.html

Mongiovi, J. (n.d.). *Hypnotic suggestion.* John Mongiovi. http://johnmongiovi.com/hypnotic-suggestion

Nichols, H. (2018, June 28). *Dreams: Causes, types, meaning, what they are, and more.* Medical News Today. https://www.medicalnewstoday.com/articles/284378#interpretations

Porter, R. (2019, April 7). *What is dream therapy?* Better Help. https://www.betterhelp.com/advice/therapy/what-is-dream-therapy/

Psychologia. (n.d.). Visual, auditory, and kinesthetic modalities. *Psychologia.* https://psychologia.co/perception-test/

Raypole, C. (2020, August 28). *Anxiety after eating: 6 possible causes.* Healthline. https://www.healthline.com/health/anxiety-after-eating

Scipioni, J. (2019, October 4). Forget self-help: Some business execs are paying up to $1,000 an hour for hypnosis. *CNBC*. https://www.cnbc.com/2019/10/04/business-leaders-turning-to-hypnosis-for-performance-help.html

Sidis, B. (n.d.). *The psychotherapeutic value of the hypnoidal state*. Sidis. https://www.sidis.net/hypnoidal.htm

Sollmann, C. M. (2016, April). *The technique of covert anchoring in hypnosis and how it is used in clinical practice*. Research Gate. https://www.researchgate.net/publication/286848312_The_T echnique_of_Covert_Anchoring_in_Hypnosis_and_How_it_is _Used_in_Clinical_Practice

Teach Me Physiology. (n.d.). *Peripheral nervous system - structure - summary*. Teach Me Physiology. https://teachmephysiology.com/nervous-system/components/peripheral-nervous-system/#:~:text=The%20SNS%20is%20responsible%20for

Time Management and Productivity. (2016). *Positive suggestion | self hypnosis techniques | What is an auto suggestion?* [Video]. YouTube. https://www.youtube.com/watch?v=pe8o234UUok

University of Chicago. (2020). *COVID response tracking study*. University of Chicago. https://www.norc.org/Research/Projects/Pages/covid-response-tracking-study.aspx

Walden University. (2021). *How positive self-talk can make you feel better and be more productive*. Walden University. https://www.waldenu.edu/online-bachelors-programs/bs-in-psychology/resource/how-positive-self-talk-can-make-you-feel-better-and-be-more-productive

Watts, T. (2021). *The depth of trance - the 4 states of hypnosis*. Self-Hypnosis. https://www.selfhypnosis.com/depth-of-trance-states/

Williamson, A. (2019). What is hypnosis and how might it work? *Palliative Care: Research and Treatment, 12.* https://doi.org/10.1177/1178224219826581

Yardley, A. (2018, March 8). Hypnotherapy for self-love – 4 important elements. *Just Imagine Therapy.* https://www.justimaginetherapy.com/hypnotherapy-for-self-love-4-important-elements/

Young, E. (2018, July 25). *Lifting the lid on the unconscious.* New Scientist. https://www.newscientist.com/article/mg23931880-400-lifting-the-lid-on-the-unconscious

Image References

Figure 10. (n.d.). Pixabay. https://pixabay.com/photos/hypnosis-self-hypnosis-suggestive-75615/

Figure Eight. (n.d.). Pixabay. https://pixabay.com/photos/morning-sunrise-woman-silhouette-2243465/

Figure Five. (n.d.). Pixabay. https://pixabay.com/illustrations/man-and-woamn-whisper-school-of-1578509/

Figure Four. (n.d.) Pixabay. https://pixabay.com/photos/candle-light-church-darkness-dark-2062861/

Figure Nine. (n.d.). Pixabay. https://pixabay.com/photos/girl-swing-rock-skyline-skyscraper-2067378/

Figure One. (n.d.). Pixabay. https://pixabay.com/photos/hypnosis-clock-pocket-watch-4041582/

Figure Seven. (n.d.). Pixabay. https://pixabay.com/photos/notebook-book-leather-leather-cover-420011/

Figure Six. (n.d.). Pixabay. https://pixabay.com/photos/staircase-spiral-architecture-600468/

Figure Three. (n.d.) Pixabay. https://pixabay.com/photos/heart-love-wave-water-association-3367962/

Made in United States
North Haven, CT
10 January 2022

14573721R00088